Cambridge Student Guide

Shakespeare

Twelfth Night

Rex Gibson

Series Editor: Rex Gibson

CAMBRIDGE
UNIVERSITY PRESS

PUBLISHED BY THE PRESS SYNDICATE OF THE UNIVERSITY OF CAMBRIDGE
The Pitt Building, Trumpington Street, Cambridge, United Kingdom

CAMBRIDGE UNIVERSITY PRESS
The Edinburgh Building, Cambridge CB2 2RU, UK
40 West 20th Street, New York, NY 10011–4211, USA
477 Williamstown Road, Port Melbourne, VIC 3207, Australia
Ruiz de Alarcón 13, 28014 Madrid, Spain
Dock House, The Waterfront, Cape Town 8001, South Africa

http://www.cambridge.org

First published 2002

Printed in the United Kingdom at the University Press, Cambridge

Typeface 9.5/12pt Scala   *System* QuarkXPress®

A catalogue record for this book is available from the British Library

ISBN 0 521 00820 4 paperback

Cover image: © Mary Evans Picture Library

Contents

Introduction

Twelfth Night. The very title seems to suggest what the play is about. Like those twelve days of celebration after Christmas, the drama will show how melancholy is challenged and dispelled by festivity. Music, fooling and carnival provide a brief, entertaining interval from the cares of the everyday world.

But Shakespeare's play is much more than escapist entertainment. It bristles with plot complications as the festive world of Sir Toby collides with the austere values of Malvolio, and Viola's generous spirit works to transform Orsino's self-indulgent romanticising. Twins are separated in shipwreck, but eventually reunited. Malvolio, the joy-hating puritan, is trapped by his own conceit, and cruelly humiliated. The seemingly affable Sir Toby Belch proves a false friend as he exploits Sir Andrew Aguecheek. Orsino and Olivia, caught up with their own emotions, reach clear-sighted understanding only at the play's end.

As *Twelfth Night* explores the foolishness that results from different kinds of love, Shakespeare stirs in a rich mix of disguise, gender ambiguity, mistaken identity and comic characters. Throughout, he ensures that inventive wordplay reveals the instability of language. Such dramatic devices are particularly suited to the play's fictional setting: Illyria.

Illyria is a never-never land of make-believe and illusion, a fantasy place full of magical possibilities, thrilling and exotic. Anything can happen there, and nothing is quite as it seems. Folly abounds. The enigmatic Feste is called 'the Fool', and the threat of madness is common. That madness has much to do with love, but for Malvolio it comes close to genuine mental derangement.

Even the play's subtitle, *What You Will*, is ambiguous. A familiar catch-phrase in Shakespeare's time, it seems to say to the audience: 'Make of it what you like, but don't take it too seriously'. Here it suggests that it is Viola's 'will' which brings happiness to Illyria.

This Guide will make you familiar with the different ways in which *Twelfth Night* has been interpreted on stage and page. It will help you see that although the play is deeply rooted in the life of Elizabethan England, it is still sharply relevant today.

Commentary

Act 1 Scene 1

> If music be the food of love, play on   (line 1)

The opening line of *Twelfth Night* establishes that love will be a central theme of the play, and that music will contribute powerfully to its mood. The vivid image suggests that love feeds off music, the sustaining food by which it grows and flourishes. The line is spoken by Orsino, Duke of Illyria, and his next lines reveal much about his character and the situation he believes himself to be in:

> Give me excess of it, that surfeiting,
> The appetite may sicken and so die.   (lines 2–3)

This is the voice of the traditional romantic lover, wallowing in his own emotions, wishing that excess might kill off his painful longings, and delight give way to disgust. Many productions strive to match the self-indulgent language with their stage picture of the scene. For example, in one production Duke Orsino lolled back extravagantly on piled cushions, surrounded by obsequious courtiers, as a small number of musicians played quietly in the background. Everyone was alert to the Duke's changeable moods, and as he commanded a particular passage to be replayed ('That strain again') the musicians dutifully repeated it and the courtiers listened attentively to their master's reaction. In another production they visibly only pretended to do so, showing the director's intention to satirise Orsino's feelings.

Orsino's response to the repeated 'strain' is again in character. He is unsatisfied by the experience, and is prompted to more thoughts on the nature of love. Those thoughts evoke another image that will run through the play: the sea. Orsino reflects that love is like the sea, which absorbs and devalues every other experience. He seems totally obsessed by his feelings, and by love itself.

Curio's question 'Will you go hunt, my lord?' is perhaps asked to try to coax Orsino out of his self-absorption. But it reveals the source of the Duke's obsession, and prompts him to yet another self-pitying image. Invited to hunt the 'hart' (deer), Orsino puns on 'heart', and declares that at the very moment he saw his love Olivia he was turned into a hart, and was pursued relentlessly by his desires. The educated members of Shakespeare's audience would recognise that the image comes from classical mythology (see page 73). The hunter Actaeon, glimpsing the goddess Diana bathing naked, was turned into a stag and pursued and killed by his own hounds. Like all that Orsino has said so far, his extreme comparison raises the question of whether he really is in love, or whether, like Romeo at the beginning of *Romeo and Juliet*, he is simply in love with the notion of love itself.

Valentine's arrival fills in the background to Orsino's melancholy. He has been sent as Orsino's messenger to Olivia, but she has refused to see him. Using the same elaborate language style as his master, Valentine reports that Olivia has vowed to remain secluded, unseen by even the sky itself, until she has mourned her dead brother for seven years.

The news prompts Orsino to yet another extravagant self-centred declaration. If she will do this for a brother, what will she do when she falls in love? He imagines thoughts of himself ('one selfsame king') passionately filling her sexual desire, thoughts and feelings ('liver, brain, and heart'). Orsino's self-regarding certainty about his own capacity to inspire love finds its final expression in his closing couplet as he proposes to indulge his love-thoughts in more romantic surroundings:

> Away before me to sweet beds of flowers:
> Love-thoughts lie rich when canopied with bowers. *(lines 40–1)*

Act 1 Scene 2

One of Shakespeare's dramatic skills is the juxtaposition of scenes. He shifts location and character, so that each new scene sheds light on the preceding one, echoing or commenting upon it. Here, Scene 2 contrasts abruptly with Scene 1. Its language style is different and it presents each new production with the challenge of staging the transition from the court of Illyria to its seashore, from thoughts of love to the consequences of a shipwreck. A few productions have staged the shipwreck itself (for example, the Trevor Nunn film, 1996, and the Royal Shakespeare Company production, 2001).

But if the contrast between the two scenes is vivid, so too are the continuities. Orsino's image of the power of the sea now becomes a real and active force, destroying a vessel and casting up a few survivors on the beach. Just as Olivia mourns her dead brother, so Viola fears her own brother, Sebastian, is lost. And in the Captain's striking image of 'Arion on the dolphin's back', music is once again seen as having power to cure. The Captain reassures Viola that Sebastian may have survived the wreck, comparing him to Arion, a legendary Greek musician who leapt overboard to escape sailors who wished to murder him. A dolphin, enchanted by Arion's music, carried him safely to shore. Once again Shakespeare uses a classical reference known to many in his own audiences, but the precise meaning of which is largely forgotten today.

Viola seems comforted, and she rewards the Captain with gold. That action, and the Captain's respectful address to her as 'lady' and 'madam', establishes her as a character of high status and wealth. She also appears very resilient, as her thoughts now turn to Illyria itself and its ruler. She and the audience now hear, for the first time, Orsino's name. How she speaks her two-line response is always deeply considered by every actress playing the role, as each decides whether they should display excessive interest in the fact he is not married:

> Orsino! I have heard my father name him.
> He was a bachelor then. *(lines 28–9)*

The Captain, born and bred in Illyria, relates the latest gossip. Orsino wishes to marry Olivia, but she, grieving for her father and her brother, has cut herself off from the sight of men and refuses to hear Orsino's messages of love. Viola recognises similarities between Olivia's grief and her own and expresses a desire to serve her, a companion in sorrow. But hearing the Captain say that Olivia has become a recluse, Viola resolves upon a different plan: she will disguise herself as a man and become an attendant to Orsino.

Viola's declaration of trust in the Captain, and her outlining of her plan, reveal another major theme of the play (and indeed of every Shakespeare play): reality and appearance. Shakespeare was concerned throughout his playwriting career with the disjunction between outward appearances and internal reality. In *Twelfth Night* that disjunction becomes not just a theme but a mainspring of the action, as character after character mistake external show for inward nature. Viola expresses the theme as she comments on the Captain's apparently trustworthy appearance:

> There is a fair behaviour in thee, captain,
> And though that nature with a beauteous wall
> Doth oft close in pollution, yet of thee
> I well believe thou hast a mind that suits
> With this thy fair and outward character.   *(lines 47–51)*

After her declaration that the Captain's outward and inward appearance are the same, Viola proposes a different condition for herself. In order to serve Orsino she will disguise her real nature, hiding her gender behind the outward appearance of a man. The confusions that arise as character after character mistake her identity will provide much of the humour and dramatic tension of the play. But, as will become evident as the action develops, Shakespeare changes his mind about one aspect of her plan. It will not be the disguised Viola, but the clown Feste who sings the songs in the play.

A few productions choose to play the first two scenes in reverse order, beginning with the shipwreck (as in *The Tempest*). But Shakespeare's own choice of dramatic juxtaposition is to begin with the self-enclosed world of Orsino's court, challenge it with the natural disaster of the shipwreck, and then make a further contrast in Scene 3 with comedy in the domestic setting of Olivia's household.

Act 1 Scene 3

After two scenes of verse, Scene 3 is entirely in prose, the conventional language style for comic episodes. Sir Toby Belch is Olivia's uncle, but he is sometimes referred to as her 'cousin', a word that Elizabethans used to describe any close relative. Toby dismissively complains that his niece's mourning prevents all enjoyment. His words express what might well be an unfeeling motto for the pleasure-loving lifestyle:

> I am sure care's an enemy to life.   *(line 2)*

Maria, Olivia's gentlewoman, warns that her mistress is much displeased with Toby's constant carousing. Toby's response suggests he may already be half-drunk or severely hungover, as he quibbles on words ('except'/'exception', 'confine'/'finer') and jokes about his boots. Maria declares that Toby's drunkenness will be his downfall, and scornfully refers to his drinking companion, Sir Andrew Aguecheek, who Toby is promoting as Olivia's wooer. Sir Toby boasts of his wealthy friend's many accomplishments, but his conversation with Maria suggests that Andrew is actually foolish, ill-educated, cowardly and gullible, and is being cheated out of his money by Sir Toby, who mockingly calls him 'Agueface'.

Sir Andrew's entrance confirms the impression. He mistakes the meaning of 'accost', believing it is Maria's name, and displays his tendency to repeat, parrot-like, whatever is said. He is mocked by Maria, whose invitation to him to 'bring your hand to th'buttery-bar and let it drink' is often accompanied on stage by an action in which she holds Andrew's hand to her breast, often to his great embarrassment. Occasionally, Sir Andrew has been played as surly, self-assured and aggressive, but such portrayals are rare, and he is conventionally portrayed as a lanky, long-haired foolish ninny, always slow on the uptake. In his confession, containing an in-joke for Shakespeare's audience that Englishmen were made stupid by eating beef, Andrew portrays his character:

> Methinks sometimes I have no more wit than a Christian or an ordinary man has, but I am a great eater of beef, and I believe that does harm to my wit. *(lines 70–2)*

Sir Andrew declares his intention to abandon his attempt to woo Olivia, and return home. Unable to understand the meaning of Toby's '*Pourquoi*' (why?), Sir Andrew reveals that his time has been spent in 'fencing, dancing, and bear-baiting'. Sir Toby's coarse sexual joke about Andrew's long straight hair ('it hangs like flax on a distaff') being spun off by a 'huswife' (prostitute) prompts him again to declare he will return home. But Andrew is easily persuaded to stay another month, with Toby's confident assurance that Olivia will certainly not marry Orsino. Andrew's words once again reveal his gullible, easily distracted nature and his delight in his own eccentricity:

I'll stay a month longer. I am a fellow o'th'strangest mind
i'th'world: I delight in masques and revels sometimes
altogether.   *(lines 92–3)*

His words give Sir Toby the opportunity both to encourage and
secretly mock his foolish friend. Andrew responds willingly to the
invitation to perform dances, as Toby extravagantly praises his
accomplishments:

Wherefore are these things hid? Wherefore have these gifts a
curtain before 'em? Are they like to take dust, like Mistress
Mall's picture? . . . Is it a world to hide virtues in? I did think,
by the excellent constitution of thy leg, it was formed under
the star of a galliard.   *(lines 102–4, 107–8)*

The scene ends with Sir Andrew capering foolishly to Sir Toby's
command. It is a telling image of the relationship of the two men, the
fat one exploiting and humiliating the skinny one who fails to see that
he is the victim of a heartless confidence trick by a seemingly jovial
friend. Appearance again does not match reality. The apparent male
camaraderie is false. Sir Toby cynically intends to fleece Sir Andrew
out of his money.

Act 1 Scene 4

Viola's plan has succeeded. Disguised as a male page, she has been in
Orsino's employment for only three days, but has already become his
favourite courtier, trusted with his confidences. Some productions use
the brief opening episode to establish that the other courtiers are
jealous of this young newcomer's success in becoming so close to
their master. In such interpretations their jealous annoyance is made
evident to Viola as Orsino bids all his other attendants to 'Stand you
awhile aloof'. They glower from a distance as Orsino talks to Viola-
Cesario.

Orsino's language is, as earlier, elaborately heightened. He has
'unclasped / To thee the book even of my secret soul' (shared his
innermost thoughts with Cesario), and his instruction to visit Olivia
becomes 'address thy gait unto her'. When Viola says that Olivia's
grief may be so strong as to deny any admittance, Orsino instructs
'him' to 'Be clamorous, and leap all civil bounds'. He urges Viola to

tell Olivia of the strength of his passion, believing that this new messenger's youth may win a hearing denied to a nuncio 'of more grave aspect'. This description probably refers to Valentine, and some productions make visible the courtier's annoyance at overhearing it.

As Orsino describes Cesario's feminine appearance the episode is rich in dramatic irony (where the audience knows something a character on stage does not). Orsino does not know he is speaking to a female when he extravagantly praises Cesario, saying how like a woman 'he' looks:

> Diana's lip
> Is not more smooth and rubious; thy small pipe
> Is as the maiden's organ, shrill and sound,
> And all is semblative a woman's part. *(lines 30–3)*

Some actors playing Orsino pause thoughtfully here, as if half-wondering about Cesario's appearance: why does 'he' look so feminine? Viola sometimes shows the audience her fear of discovery, but the moment quickly passes. For Shakespeare's audience there was an additional level of irony, because at that time only males were allowed to act. So Viola-Cesario was a boy, playing a girl, playing a boy!

Once again, the silent courtiers have an opportunity to respond to Cesario as Orsino bids them 'Some four or five attend him – / All if you will'. Again, some productions make it clear that the courtiers regard Viola-Cesario as the cuckoo in the nest who has replaced any influence they might have had with their master. Orsino's self-centredness is confirmed as he declares like the stereotypical melancholy romantic lover 'for I myself am best / When least in company' (an expression that recalls Romeo's mood at the start of *Romeo and Juliet*). Much of what the audience has seen so far of Orsino raises a puzzling question of just what it is that makes him so attractive to the clear-thinking, witty Viola. As she leaves to act as Orsino's messenger to woo Olivia, her final couplet reveals that she has fallen head over heels in love with him:

> I'll do my best
> To woo your lady. [*Aside*] Yet a barful strife!
> Whoe'er I woo, myself would be his wife. *(lines 39–41)*

Act 1 Scene 5

The scene returns to Olivia's household where Maria warns Feste that he is in trouble for his absence. Feste does not take her scolding seriously, and the two characters engage in punning and wordplay that is anchored firmly in the humour and life of Elizabethan England. Today, the actors sometimes deliver the cross-talk accompanied with actions and gestures to help modern audiences understand the jokes. For example, in one production Feste grasped his crotch to bring out the sexual implication of 'Many a good hanging prevents a bad marriage'. In another Maria showed how Feste's breeches ('gaskins') would fall if his 'points' (braces) broke. Their repartee ends with an exchange hinting that Maria and Sir Toby are having an affair.

Each of the previous four scenes has established the importance of Olivia. Now the audience gets its first sight of her, accompanied by her steward Malvolio (who has not been mentioned before). On stage she often appears a grave, dignified figure dressed head to foot in black, the emblem of deep mourning. However, as will soon become clear, appearance is again deceptive, and a very different impression of Olivia emerges. But for now, Feste seems apprehensive about how he will be treated by her. The abruptness of Olivia's first words suggest that he will need all his witty skills to escape dismissal or punishment. His response seems breath-takingly impudent:

> OLIVIA Take the fool away.
> FESTE Do you not hear, fellows? Take away the lady.
>
> *(lines 31–2)*

Feste's attempt at humour meets with little success as Olivia calls him 'a dry fool', declares she will have no more of him, and accuses him of dishonesty. Feste deflects the criticism, using what seems a carefully constructed philosophical argument to prove how he might amend. He ends by repeating his impertinent order:

> The lady bade take away the fool; therefore I say again, take
> her away. *(lines 42–3)*

To Olivia's rebuke, Feste quotes a Latin phrase that implies it is a mistake to judge a person by appearances ('the hood does not make the monk'). Feste's official title may be Fool, but he is by no means foolish. He reminds Olivia that although he may be dressed in motley as a jester, he has all his wits about him: 'I wear not motley in my brain'. His statements are further instances of the theme of the difference between appearance and reality. He asks for leave to prove Olivia a fool. The fact that Olivia grants permission suggests that her commitment to a life of mourning is not so strong as earlier report and her appearance may have implied. There is a striking contrast between her outward show, all in black, and her willingness to answer Feste's questions about her brother's death.

Feste's 'proof' is dazzlingly simple. Only a fool would mourn a brother whose soul is in heaven, not hell. There is often a long fraught pause as everyone on stage waits to see how Olivia will respond to Feste's effrontery. She does not reply directly, but her question to Malvolio suggests she is not offended, and may be amused. Malvolio dismisses Feste contemptuously. Feste's equally sharp retort implies that Sir Toby thinks little of Malvolio. On stage, Olivia often seems to enjoy the hostility between the two men, which could explain why she invites Malvolio to reply. His supercilious response scathingly disapproves of her, Feste, and her father who enjoyed Feste's humour:

> I marvel your ladyship takes delight in such a barren rascal . . .
> I protest I take these wise men that crow so at these set kind of
> fools no better than the fools' zanies.   *(lines 67, 71–2)*

Malvolio's sour and humiliating rebuke expresses what his name implies ('Malvolio' = ill-wishing), and it evokes Olivia's criticism. She condemns his attitude, and urges greater charity and generosity of spirit. She excuses Feste as an 'allowed fool'. Her character description of Malvolio not only echoes the play's recurring connection of love and food, but will prove remarkably perceptive as the play develops:

> O you are sick of self-love, Malvolio, and taste with a
> distempered appetite.   *(lines 73–4)*

Maria's entry heralds the arrival of a 'young gentleman' (Viola disguised as Cesario), who is being delayed by Sir Toby. Olivia despatches Malvolio to dismiss the unwanted messenger, then gently rebukes Feste. Sir Toby, quite drunk, makes a brief appearance, muddling his words and justifying his name as he blames his belching on pickled herrings. Olivia sends Feste to care for her drunken kinsman, and then hears Malvolio's protestation that the newly arrived messenger from Orsino absolutely refuses to leave until he has spoken with her. Malvolio's description of the disguised Viola catches the sexually ambiguous nature of her appearance:

> Not yet old enough for a man, nor young enough for a boy: as a squash is before 'tis a peascod, or a codling when 'tis almost an apple. 'Tis with him in standing water, between boy and man. He is very well-favoured and he speaks very shrewishly. One would think his mother's milk were scarce out of him.
>
> *(lines 130–4)*

The description intrigues Olivia. Probably to Malvolio's surprise, she commands the messenger be allowed entry. Maria is ordered to veil her mistress, and Olivia prepares to hear this new messenger from Orsino. Once again, Olivia does not display the behaviour appropriate to someone in deep mourning. She is quite unlike the 'cloistress' described in Scene 1, as she playfully requests Cesario to speak to her as 'The honourable lady of the house'. Viola begins her prepared address in high style, which recalls Orsino's manner: 'Most radiant, exquisite, and unmatchable beauty', but is disconcerted by not knowing if it is really Olivia to whom she speaks. Her attempt to discover which woman is Olivia is full of the language of the theatre ('speech', 'con', 'studied', 'part'), and prompts Olivia to ask playfully if this well-spoken young man is an actor: 'Are you a comedian?'

The verbal fencing that follows shows Viola possesses both a lively wit and proud confidence about her own status. She courteously criticises Olivia ('you do usurp yourself'), jokingly fends off Maria's attempt to remove her ('No, good swabber'), defends her 'rudeness' of behaviour as something learned from her hosts, and intriguingly declares her identity and message 'as secret as maidenhead'. Ever more interested, Olivia dismisses Maria and her other attendants and teasingly questions Viola-Cesario about his 'text': Orsino's message. Viola responds in the same style, but then asks to see Olivia's face. On stage, Olivia sometimes removes her veil with a deliberate flirtatiousness, obviously fascinated by this unusual young man, and looking for a compliment: 'Is't not well done?' Viola's reply is deflating, but Olivia insists that her beauty is natural:

VIOLA   Excellently done, if God did all.
OLIVIA   'Tis in grain, sir; 'twill endure wind and weather.

(lines 193–4)

Viola uses verse to praise Olivia's beauty, but accuses her of cruelty if she refuses to reproduce it by having children. Her accusation echoes the theme of Shakespeare's *Sonnets 1–17*, which attempt to persuade a young man to marry and have children. Olivia's mocking reply promises to leave various lists ('divers schedules') itemising all the elements of her beauty. Viola's blunt response accuses Olivia of pride, and tells of Orsino's intense love for her. Olivia acknowledges Orsino's many fine qualities but asserts (twice) that she cannot love him. Viola-Cesario protests that if 'he' suffered such tortures of passion that Orsino endures, Olivia's reply would be incomprehensible. Olivia's demand 'Why, what would you?' prompts Viola to speak some of Shakespeare's best-known love poetry as she tells how every action would express her love and move Olivia to pity:

> Make me a willow cabin at your gate,
> And call upon my soul within the house;
> Write loyal cantons of contemnèd love,
> And sing them loud even in the dead of night;
> Hallow your name to the reverberate hills,
> And make the babbling gossip of the air
> Cry out 'Olivia!' O you should not rest
> Between the elements of air and earth
> But you should pity me!   *(lines 223–31)*

The soaring lyricism entrances Olivia. Her half line 'You might do much' expresses how much Viola's words have affected her (although on stage she sometimes speaks the four words with cool irony, as if she is keeping up her guard, unwilling to show how much she is attracted to this eloquent young man). She questions Viola-Cesario about 'his' parents, and receives an enigmatic reply: 'Above my fortunes, yet my state is well: / I am a gentleman.' She declares she cannot love Orsino, but implies that Viola must return to her to report the Duke's reaction. Viola disdainfully rejects an offered fee, and prophetically wishes that when Olivia falls in love, she too will experience the similar hard-hearted contempt of rejection.

In her soliloquy Olivia fears she has fallen in love with Cesario. She thinks of 'him' as 'thou', an Elizabethan style of addressing someone who was especially close or loved. The familiar pronoun contrasts with 'you', a more distant form of address that she had used throughout their conversation. She judges Cesario to be a gentleman by his 'five-fold blazon' (see page 78) and appears to wish that Orsino were Cesario ('Unless the master were the man'). Unaware that she has fallen in love with a woman disguised as a man, Olivia sends Malvolio on a false errand to ensure that Cesario returns tomorrow. Malvolio is to return a ring that Olivia falsely claims Cesario has left behind. She is well and truly snared by Viola's outward appearance, and fears what may happen, but resolves that she must leave the outcome to fate to decide:

> Fate, show thy force; ourselves we do not owe.
> What is decreed must be; and be this so. *(lines 265–6)*

Act 1: Critical review

In Act 1 Shakespeare's dazzling juxtaposition of scenes, characters and situations quickly establishes the strange world of Illyria. The fast-moving scene changes have a cinematic quality: the emotional hothouse of Orsino's court, the shipwrecked survivors, the revelling of Sir Toby and Sir Andrew. The act ends with the varied events in Olivia's household: Feste's wordplay, Malvolio's disdain, and the fraught encounter between Olivia and the disguised Viola.

The changes of location are accompanied by a similarly wide range of characters and moods: Orsino's self-indulgent love, Viola's resourcefulness, Sir Toby's covert mocking of Sir Andrew, Andrew's gullibility, Feste's edgy humour, Malvolio's arrogance, Olivia's readiness to abandon her mourning. The act ends in a complex love tangle: Viola loves Orsino, but must woo Olivia on his behalf, and Olivia has fallen in love with Viola, believing her to be a man.

There is similar variety in the language of the act. It alternates between the lyrical and the satirical. It ranges from the romantic to the coarse. It is sometimes sincere, sometimes mocking. And in the recurring image of the changeability of the sea, it echoes the unreliability that characterises all aspects of Illyria.

But for all the variation, Shakespeare ensures that all characters share something in common. All are affected in some way by the difference between appearance and reality. In their self-obsession, both Orsino and Olivia mistakenly fantasise about their conception of love. Sir Toby deceitfully feeds Sir Andrew's notion of himself as a talented lover, dancer and man of the world. Malvolio seems incapable of recognising or practising humour or generosity.

Two characters possess the ability to see beyond the limitations of mere appearances. Feste wittily displays the skill he will use throughout the play as he exploits the instability of language. Viola also deliberately exploits the difference between outward appearance and inward reality when she adopts a disguise as the male Cesario.

The consequences of Viola's disguise, as other characters mistake her appearance, will be Shakespeare's dramatic device to complicate, but finally resolve, the love tangles of the play. By the end of Act 1, Shakespeare has established the major relationships in that tangle.

Act 2 Scene 1

Two new characters appear in this scene, which contains strong echoes of Act 1 Scene 2. In that earlier scene, Viola had been rescued from the shipwreck by the Captain. Now it is revealed that Antonio has similarly rescued Viola's twin brother Sebastian. Like his sister, Sebastian intends to journey to Orsino's court; and just as the Captain promised to help Viola, so Antonio wishes to be servant to Sebastian. In both scenes each twin expresses sorrow for the other whom they believe drowned. And just as Viola proposed to disguise herself, so Sebastian seems to have assumed a new identity as Roderigo.

Virtually all productions add a further similarity with Act 1 by having Sebastian dressed identically to Viola in her disguise as Cesario. They also often show that Sebastian possesses the same hairstyle, gestures, expressions and manner of speech as his sister. How far an actual physical likeness should be achieved is a matter for debate, and most productions accept that the twins, a boy and a girl, cannot be identical.

However, Shakespeare ensures that the two scenes contain differences that will enhance dramatic effect. Sebastian rejects Antonio's offer of help, and possesses no clear plan of what he might do. His complex sentence 'My determinate voyage is mere extravagancy' seems simply to mean 'My plan for travel is only for wandering'. Most significant is Antonio's feeling for Sebastian. In the earlier scene the Captain willingly helps Viola, then disappears for ever from the play (though he will be heard of in the final scene, see page 52). But Antonio, a somewhat mysterious character, has developed an intense affection, even love, for Sebastian, and some productions stress the homoeroticism of the scene (as, for example, in the 2001 Royal Shakespeare Company production). Despite the dangers Antonio faces in Illyria, he determines to follow Sebastian. His brief soliloquy hints at the dramatic consequences that will flow from his decision:

> I have many enemies in Orsino's court,
> Else would I very shortly see thee there.
> But come what may, I do adore thee so
> That danger shall seem sport, and I will go.   *(lines 33–6)*

Act 2 Scene 2

This scene, in which Malvolio gives Olivia's ring to Viola, is sometimes played before Scene 1. That staging makes it immediately follow the final scene of Act 1 in which Olivia despatched Malvolio on his errand. He often arrives out of breath and irritated, and delivers his message in short bursts with petulant disdain. Viola's reaction tells much about her character. She quickly realises that Olivia is engaged in a pretence, but she tells an untruth of her own to ensure that Malvolio does not become aware of his mistress' deceit:

> She took the ring of me. I'll none of it. *(line 10)*

Malvolio falls for the lie and, probably irritated by the confidence of this uppish young man, adds an embellishment of his own: 'you peevishly threw it to her'. In each new production, the actor playing Malvolio seeks to find an effective way of returning the ring in a manner that matches his personality. For example, in one production he slipped it over his long staff of office and with a mixture of contempt and dignity let it slide down to Viola's feet as he spoke 'Receive it so.'

Viola's soliloquy, simply expressed but full of perplexity, surprise and change of thought, has become one of Shakespeare's best-known set pieces, often used as an audition piece or performed extract. On stage it invariably works effectively with Viola candidly sharing her thoughts with the audience, taking them into her confidence, reasoning her way through the lines, step by step. She knows that the ring is a trick, but what game is Olivia playing? Viola expresses wonderment as she realises the consequence of her disguise as Cesario. Appearance has triumphed over reality, and Olivia has fallen for her: 'She loves me sure'. The thought makes her feel affectionate pity for Olivia and declare how the devil ('pregnant enemy') works through false appearance:

> Poor lady, she were better love a dream.
> Disguise, I see thou art a wickedness,
> Wherein the pregnant enemy does much. *(lines 23–5)*

Reflecting on how easily women are tricked by insincere handsome deceivers ('proper-false'), Viola wonders how this complicated triangle will work out: Orsino loves Olivia, Viola loves Orsino, and Olivia loves the disguised Viola. At the end of Act 1, Olivia had trusted to fate to work out her emotional dilemma. Now Viola puts her trust in time to unravel the complexity of her situation in the bewildering world of Illyria:

> O time, thou must untangle this, not I;
> It is too hard a knot for me t'untie.   *(lines 37–8)*

Act 2 Scene 3

It is very late at night at Olivia's house, and Sir Toby and Sir Andrew have been drinking heavily. They talk together in the apparently logical but laboured and befuddled way that characterises drunks, each man making statements he considers profoundly true. Toby uses a Latin tag to praise the healthiness of rising at dawn. He corrects Andrew's reply, but then, perhaps recalling there is more money to swindle out of his foolish friend, elaborately praises his wisdom in saying life consists of eating and drinking. He calls to Maria for wine, but it is Feste who enters.

Feste's seemingly enigmatic question 'Did you never see the picture of 'We Three'?' challenges the actors to invent 'business' to create a stage image of the picture of three fools (a well-known Elizabethan inn sign of two fools, with the spectator making a third). Andrew's foolishness becomes even more evident as he praises Feste's 'gracious fooling' the previous night. He does not recognise the mockery in Feste's nonsensical response, and calls for a song. Feste accepts money from the two knights, but brusquely interrupts Sir Andrew's attempt to explain his reason for the gift. Feste's love song begins with the hope of love, but its second verse is poignantly bitter-sweet:

> O mistress mine, where are you roaming?
> O stay and hear, your true love's coming,
>   That can sing both high and low.
> Trip no further, pretty sweeting;
> Journeys end in lovers meeting,
>   Every wise man's son doth know.

What is love? 'Tis not hereafter;
Present mirth hath present laughter;
    What's to come is still unsure.
In delay there lies no plenty,
Then come kiss me, sweet and twenty;
    Youth's a stuff will not endure.   *(lines 33–8, 41–6)*

The themes of love and music are evident in the song, and the second verse's sense of seizing the all-too-rapidly passing moment contributes powerfully to the yearning, autumnal mood some productions strive to create for the play. The song seems both appropriate and inappropriate to the two listening men. Sir Andrew might take the first verse as predicting he will win Olivia, but the melancholy uncertainty of the second downbeat verse is far less optimistic. It temporarily lulls the two knights into reflective appreciation of Feste's 'mellifluous' and 'contagious' voice. But the quiet mood quickly passes as Sir Toby demands:

But shall we make the welkin dance indeed? Shall we rouse
the night owl in a catch that will draw three souls out of one
weaver? Shall we do that?   *(lines 50–3)*

And that is just what they do. Stage productions have presented the singing in all kinds of ways, and most develop into a raucous, riotous celebration that justifies Maria's description of it as 'caterwauling'. She pleads with them to be quiet, and warns that Olivia has called for Malvolio to stop their din. But prompted by Sir Toby's dismissal of Olivia and her steward, the three men carry on regardless, creating mounting confusion. Much to Maria's despair, the noise usually becomes deafening, and the behaviour more wild. The celebration builds to a climax, and Malvolio's entry, sometimes in a nightgown and nightcap, sometimes with his hair in curlers, but still wearing his chain of office, is a hugely enjoyable dramatic moment. He remonstrates with the revellers:

My masters, are you mad? Or what are you? Have you no wit,
manners, nor honesty but to gabble like tinkers at this time of
night? . . . Is there no respect of place, persons, nor time in
you?   *(lines 75–7, 79)*

Malvolio's rebuke is in vain. Sir Toby puns on his words and dismisses him with 'Sneck up!' Malvolio, probably greatly offended, delivers another rebuke, this time to Sir Toby, telling that Olivia wishes him to reform or leave her house. That rebuke is equally unsuccessful, and Sir Toby and Feste increasingly ridicule Malvolio with snatches of songs. Sir Toby's final insult expresses contempt for Malvolio's low social status, and for all puritanically minded killjoys who condemn drinking and revelry:

> Art any more than a steward? Dost thou think because thou art
> virtuous there shall be no more cakes and ale?   *(lines 97–9)*

With a final warning to Maria, Malvolio leaves, pursued by another of Sir Toby's humiliating reminders of his low status: 'Go, sir, rub your chain with crumbs.' Sir Andrew displays his usual foolishness in empty threats against Malvolio, but Maria has a more practical plan to trick the overbearing steward who threatens to report unfavourably on her to Olivia. She condemns Malvolio as a puritan and a social climber who believes he has excellent qualities that make people love him. That self-regard will be the means by which his downfall is achieved. Maria will forge a letter, supposedly from Olivia, praising and expressing love for Malvolio. His high opinion of himself will make him believe it, and so expose him to ridicule. The trap for Malvolio is beginning to be set.

The scene ends with the prospect of further drinking and with another example of Sir Toby's deceit. He plans to extract more money from Sir Andrew by convincing him that he will successfully win Olivia. Sir Andrew, ever the ninny, agrees. But a few moments earlier, Andrew has a memorable opportunity to evoke audience sympathy. Hearing Sir Toby boast that Maria adores him (Toby), Andrew can create a touching moment of wistful tender-sweet memory as he recalls:

> I was adored once, too.   *(line 153)*

Act 2 Scene 4

After the riotous singing of the previous scene, music is once more the theme, but in a quite different key. Orsino calls for music to cheer him, and sends for Feste to sing an old song he had sung the night before. As the musicians play, Orsino shares his thoughts with Viola. He claims he is the model of all true lovers, because Olivia is constantly in his mind. Once again there is a feeling of obsessive indulgence in his language. It can sound self-centred and boastful, suggesting he is philosophising about love, rather than genuinely experiencing it. He praises Viola's judgement of the tune the musicians are playing:

> It gives a very echo to the seat
> Where love is throned.   *(lines 19–20)*

Impressed by Viola-Cesario's words, Orsino questions whether 'he' has ever loved, and Viola hints at her true feelings by saying she once loved someone of Orsino's complexion and age. The reply prompts Orsino to more reflections on love. He pompously advises that women should marry men older than themselves, because men are fickle (a statement in direct contradiction to what he said only moments ago) and women, like briefly-flowering roses, soon lose their looks. Viola's reply can create a poignant moment of theatre, as she agrees that women's perfection all too quickly fades:

> And so they are. Alas, that they are so:
> To die, even when they to perfection grow!   *(lines 38–9)*

Feste arrives, and Orsino's demand for the love song evokes a nostalgic image of women and girls spinning and weaving outside their houses, singing as they worked. Critics often comment that the image recalls the familiar sight of clothworkers and lacemakers in Elizabethan England, but also sometimes remark that it is yet another example of Orsino's dreamy fantasies about love.

If a director's intention is to create an atmosphere tinged with melancholy, Feste's song provides rich opportunities with its powerful rhymes and repetitions, and imagery of death. It tells of a true lover who died for love and who wished to be forgotten. It seems perfectly fitted to Orsino's mood, but there is the possibility that Feste may be mocking, rather than merely reflecting the Duke's introverted, changeable feelings. That suspicion of mockery deepens as Feste accompanies his acceptance of money from Orsino ('There's for thy pains') with a scarcely veiled rebuke: 'No pains, sir, I take pleasure in singing, sir'. The impression may be confirmed as Feste impertinently wishes 'the melancholy god' to protect Orsino, wishes the Duke to wear taffeta (a silk which changes colour) and describes his mind as 'a very opal', a jewel which seems to change colour.

But any hint of criticism or irony seems lost on Orsino, and he orders Viola once more to take his message of love to Olivia, 'yond same sovereign cruelty'. When Viola hints at her own love for Orsino by suggesting some lady might love him as intensely as he loves Olivia, Orsino arrogantly claims that his capacity for love is greater than that of any woman. As Viola persists, the audience recognises that she is describing herself, and that she is very close to revealing her disguise when she tells him that:

> My father had a daughter loved a man
> As it might be perhaps, were I a woman,
> I should your lordship. *(lines 103–5)*

Orsino asks what happened to the 'daughter' who loved so intensely. Viola's account contains perhaps the most famous set of images in the play:

> She never told her love,
> But let concealment like a worm i'th'bud
> Feed on her damask cheek. She pined in thought,
> And with a green and yellow melancholy
> She sat like Patience on a monument,
> Smiling at grief. *(lines 106–11)*

Viola replies ambiguously to Orsino's enquiry whether her 'sister' died of her love: she is 'all the daughters of my father's house'. With her mind on Sebastian, she adds 'And all the brothers, too'. Orsino is caught up in Viola's story, but does he suspect that his page is not really what 'he' seems? It is a crucial episode in the development of both characters. Every production works out its own version of how closely Orsino pays attention to Viola's appearance, and many suggest his growing affection for his young page. But the scene ends with Viola switching Orsino's thoughts back to Olivia. His closing couplet is again much in character, assertively confident of the overwhelming power of his love:

> To her in haste; give her this jewel; say
> My love can give no place, bide no denay.   *(lines 120–1)*

Act 2 Scene 5

The gulling (duping) of Malvolio is about to begin, and a new character appears, Fabian. In Act 2 Scene 3 Maria had planned that Feste would eavesdrop on the trickery, together with Sir Toby and Sir Andrew. But now Feste is not involved (possibly biding his time to exact a more cruel revenge), and Fabian takes his place. Who is he? A servant, or one of the gentlemen hangers-on found in many Elizabethan households? Shakespeare does not make it clear, but reveals that Fabian has a grudge against Malvolio, who reported him to Olivia for bear-baiting on her property. The echoes of Elizabethan England are again very strong here, in a reminder that the puritans objected strongly to bear-baiting. Whoever he is, Fabian looks forward to enjoying Malvolio's humiliation.

Maria warns that Malvolio is approaching, preening himself mightily. She orders the three men 'into the box-tree' to watch. In Shakespeare's own theatre it seems probable that the 'box-tree' was a simple stage property. Today, every new production of *Twelfth Night* spends much time in rehearsal working out just how the men should conceal themselves to increase audience enjoyment. Maria places her forged letter down. The trap is set, and Malvolio, like a fish lulled into false security by gentle stroking, will be caught by flattery:

> here comes the trout that must be caught with tickling.
>
>   *(lines 18–19)*

Malvolio's soliloquising reveals just how susceptible he is to flattery. Maria has judged him well. Up to this moment he has shown little or nothing of the private fantasies that lie behind his austere appearance. But now he day-dreams aloud, and shows that his self-regard conceals exotic passions and ambitions. On stage, he usually talks to himself in a kind of reverie, rather than, as with most other Shakespearean soliloquies, sharing his thoughts directly with the audience. To the increasing fury of Sir Toby, Malvolio fantasises about what might be. He persuades himself that Olivia loves him, and that through marriage to her, his social rank has risen to become Count Malvolio. He hints at their sexual relationship and imagines himself, in his new high status, regarding his household with a cold and superior stare, and sending for Sir Toby.

Toby's rage is barely controllable. He punctuates Malvolio's imaginings with insults, oaths and threats. On stage the episode can be hilarious as Toby and Andrew come dangerously close to revealing themselves as they express their indignation. Fabian constantly restrains them, and his image of Malvolio as a puffed-up male bird boastfully displaying its plumage aptly describes how Malvolio behaves as he enjoys his secret fantasies:

> Contemplation makes a rare turkey-cock of him; how he jets
> under his advanced plumes!   (lines 26–7)

Malvolio makes a momentary slip as he enjoys the prospect of waiting disdainfully for Sir Toby. He imagines playing with his steward's seal of office, but suddenly remembers he is 'Count Malvolio', and turns the unspoken 'seal' into 'some rich jewel'. As he relishes the prospect of frostily treating Toby as a social inferior and reproving him to reform his drinking, Toby almost explodes; but Sir Andrew recognises all too clearly and accepts Malvolio's description of him as 'a foolish knight'. Shakespeare's masterly handling of dialogue and dramatic effect enables actors to make the scene an episode of hugely enjoyable theatre. It invariably works effectively on stage, and Shakespeare ratchets up the level of enjoyment by having Malvolio discover the forged letter (in one production, sticking to the sole of his foot):

> What employment have we here?
> . . .
> By my life, this is my lady's hand   (lines 68, 72)

Malvolio believes he recognises Olivia's handwriting, and Shakespeare gives him and Sir Andrew an obscene joke ('cut' was Elizabethan slang for the female genitals). The fact that Andrew doesn't get it becomes part of the joke. Maria's trick succeeds brilliantly, and the intriguing contents of the poem, with its strong hints ('I may command where I adore') and the letters M.O.A.I. send Malvolio into a delirium of speculation, convincing himself that Olivia is declaring her love for him. Once again this 'figuring out' exercise by Malvolio, punctuated by mocking comments from Sir Toby and Fabian, provides rich opportunities for comic business in performance.

Malvolio's reading of the prose letter offers further comic opportunities (not least in the hackneyed, but still funny action of revolving in response to the command 'revolve'). Many actors read the letter slowly, section by section, accompanying each with responsive actions and expressions (and with the three overhearers also reacting with gleeful mimes). Malvolio's conviction that he is the object of Olivia's desire grows stronger with each sentence, and he revels in the inviting possibility that seems so obviously offered him by his mistress:

> In my stars I am above thee, but be not afraid of greatness.
> Some are born great, some achieve greatness, and some have
> greatness thrust upon 'em.   *(lines 119–21)*

The lines will eventually return to haunt him, but at this moment he is overjoyed. When he reads 'let me see thee a steward still', he knows he is the man! He resolves to do just as the letter instructs, to be surly with servants, 'opposite' with Sir Toby, and to talk loudly and confidently of politics: 'tang arguments of state' ('tang' means 'ring out like a bell'). Most deliciously for the audience, he resolves to appear in yellow stockings and cross-gartered to woo Olivia. Shakespeare provides the prospect of further humiliation in store for the sober-sided steward as he finds a postscript that tells him to smile as he next meets Olivia. Like a trout truly caught with tickling, he resolves to do so, often engaging in a long, hilarious struggle to force his features, unaccustomed to any expression but haughty seriousness, into the unfamiliar rictus of a smile:

> Jove, I thank thee. I will smile; I will do every thing that thou
> wilt have me.   *(lines 146–7)*

Sir Toby and the others are delighted with the success of Maria's device, and Sir Andrew foolishly echoes all that Toby says in praise of her. Maria's words foretell the embarrassment for Malvolio and the pleasure for the audience that lie ahead when Malvolio meets Olivia:

> He will come to her in yellow stockings, and 'tis a colour she abhors, and cross-gartered, a fashion she detests; and he will smile upon her, which will now be so unsuitable to her disposition, being addicted to a melancholy as she is, that it cannot but turn him into a notable contempt.　　*(lines 165–9)*

Act 2: Critical review

After the different portrayals of love in Act 1, Shakespeare now invites the audience to consider yet another kind of passionate attachment. The nature of Antonio's feelings for Sebastian, 'I do adore thee so', has long puzzled critics. Is it a dramatisation of the intense male friendships common in Elizabethan England? Is it a homosexual attachment? Whatever its nature, it will have dramatic consequences as Antonio decides to follow Sebastian to Orsino's court.

Once again the play's preoccupation with the difference between appearance and reality is evident in every scene. Sebastian calls himself Roderigo; Viola realises that her disguise has caused Olivia to fall in love with her; Toby's revelling has melancholy undertones; Maria plans to trap Malvolio by a forged letter; Orsino continues to deceive himself in his fantasies about the incomparable quality of his love. But the most obvious and most hilarious example of the mismatch of outward appearance and inward reality occurs in Scene 5. The seemingly austere Malvolio has secret passions, but is totally unable to perceive the unreality of his own self-image, his expectations, or the letter he reads. His failure to see things as they truly are will have both comic and cruelly humiliating outcomes.

The act provides uncomfortable reminders of misogynistic male attitudes. Viola reflects how women's 'frailty' makes them easily deceived by false appearance. Orsino regrets the brevity of women's beauty and dismisses their love as fickle 'appetite'. Even Malvolio's fantasies about Olivia seem much concerned with her as a possession, a route to wealth and high social status. That concern for social class also finds expression in subtle reminders by Sebastian and Viola of their high status, and starkly in Toby's contemptuous dismissal of Malvolio: 'Art any more than a steward?'

Feste's two songs contain powerful reminders of the sadness that lies behind love. The first ends with the reminder that 'Youth's a stuff will not endure'. The second poignantly conveys the conventional image of romantic melancholy: the lover who dies from rejection by 'a fair cruel maid'. The sombre sense of the corrosive effects of time in each song sharply contrasts with Viola's resolution that time will untangle the love knot in which she is caught.

Act 3 Scene 1

The meeting between Viola and Feste gives insight into how Shakespeare enjoyed drawing attention to the slipperiness of language in the context of theatre. Feste refuses to give a straight answer. He seizes every opportunity to exploit the ambiguity of language, to show how different possible meanings of words can twist answers in quite different directions from those expected. The most obvious example (which some critics consider laboured as Feste spells out the pun) is in the first exchange:

VIOLA   Dost thou live by thy tabor?
FESTE   No, sir, I live by the church.
VIOLA   Art thou a churchman?
FESTE   No such matter, sir. I do live by the church; for I do live at
        my house, and my house doth stand by the church.

(lines 1–5)

Viola joins in the language game, and the episode bristles with phrases that emphasise the equivocal nature of language: 'words are very rascals', 'words are grown so false'. Feste describes himself, not as Olivia's Fool, but as 'her corrupter of words'. His mocking comment on how words can be twisted is sometimes taken as Shakespeare's own view of language (partly because some critics believe that Shakespeare helped his father, a glovemaker, to make soft leather 'cheveril' gloves):

> To see this age! A sentence is but a cheveril glove to a good wit
> – how quickly the wrong side may be turned outward!

(lines 9–11)

Feste continues his word-juggling as he talks Viola into giving him money. Within his joking is evidence of Shakespeare's interest in literature and theatre. Feste's allusion to Pandarus recalls the classical Greek love story of Troilus and Cressida (see page 73), which, a few years after *Twelfth Night*, Shakespeare would dramatise. Even Feste's puzzling mention of 'element' may refer to Shakespeare's contemporary playwright, Ben Jonson, who was mocked for his fondness for the word. Viola's soliloquy (lines 50–8) is thought by some to be Shakespeare's tribute to Robert Armin, the actor who first played Feste (see pages 66–7). It praises the really good jester who suits his humour to the particular audience and occasion, rather than cracking jokes about everything.

This seemingly self-contained opening sequence of the scene sets interesting character puzzles. What is the attitude of each character to the other? How do they relate to each other? (In a few productions it is evident that Feste sees through Viola's disguise.) What is Feste's attitude to his role as a 'corrupter of words'? A range of different, equally valid answers are possible. But the episode also contains a reminder of the love plot, as Viola remarks that she is sick for a beard, but in a wry aside to the audience reveals that it is Orsino's she has in mind. That love plot now returns to centre stage as, after Viola's brief punning encounter with Sir Andrew and Sir Toby, she greets Olivia fulsomely. Her elaborate words are envied by Sir Andrew who resolves to use them in his own wooing:

> 'Odours', 'pregnant', and 'vouchsafed': I'll get 'em all three all
> ready.   *(lines 76–7)*

Much to Andrew's discomfiture, Olivia orders everyone away, so that she may be left alone with Viola-Cesario. She takes both 'his' hand and the initiative. It becomes quickly evident that Olivia intends to reveal her true feelings for this attractive youth. She asks 'his' name, rejects the thought that he might be her servant, and dismisses all talk of Orsino. There is something else she would rather hear, more wonderful 'Than music from the spheres' (the heavenly music that many Elizabethans believed was made as the planets rotated in concentric crystal spheres).

Olivia admits that the ring she sent was a trick, 'shameful cunning'. Seeming to blame Viola, Olivia uses an image from bear-baiting ('stake', 'baited', 'unmuzzled') to describe how her secret love for Cesario tears at her. She declares her feelings are clearly visible: 'a cypress (thin linen), not a bosom, / Hides my heart'. Viola, possibly deeply troubled by the confession, says she pities Olivia, but that her pity is not love. Olivia's image of the lion and the wolf pictures Viola as a predator. She seems to accept that she cannot have 'him', but then asks for Cesario's opinion of her. The resulting exchange is a torrent of monosyllabic words that give additional force to each statement that appearance does not match reality:

OLIVIA   I prithee tell me what thou think'st of me.
VIOLA   That you do think you are not what you are.
OLIVIA   If I think so, I think the same of you.
VIOLA   Then think you right: I am not what I am.
OLIVIA   I would you were as I would have you be.   *(lines 123–7)*

In Shakespeare's time, Viola's 'I am not what I am' would have been spoken by a boy playing a girl playing a boy. That fact made the words even more rich in dramatic irony than today, when the part is played by a female. But even today, dramatic irony is still strongly present because the audience knows that Olivia is unaware that the 'man' she thinks she is wooing is actually a woman in disguise. Admiring Viola's beauty, and overwhelmed by her own feelings, Olivia cannot hold back from an open declaration of love:

> Cesario, by the roses of the spring,
> By maidhood, honour, truth, and everything,
> I love thee so that, maugre all thy pride,
> Nor wit nor reason can my passion hide.   *(lines 134–7)*

Olivia uses further lyrical rhyming couplets to argue for Viola to receive her love. Viola replies in the same verse pattern, but truthfully declares that no woman has, or ever will have, her heart save she herself alone. But Olivia begs her to return and, in an ambiguous final couplet which might also refer to Orsino, hopes that Viola's feelings towards her may change from hate to love:

> Yet come again: for thou perhaps mayst move
> That heart which now abhors to like his love.   *(lines 148–9)*

Act 3 Scene 2

More of Sir Andrew's gullibility is about to be revealed. He begins by declaring vehemently that he will leave Illyria. He is convinced he cannot win Olivia, because with his own eyes he has seen her behave more affectionately towards Cesario than she has ever behaved towards him. He explodes angrily, suspecting he is being mocked (he is) as Fabian claims that Olivia's behaviour shows she really loves him. But, true to his nature, Andrew readily and foolishly accepts the preposterous explanation: Olivia flirts with Cesario in order to provoke Sir Andrew to a show of bravery. He should have joked with her and so struck Cesario dumb. The fact that Andrew did not do so has much displeased her:

> you are now sailed into the north of my lady's opinion, where
> you will hang like an icicle on a Dutchman's beard
>
> *(lines 20–2)*

Fabian's image would remind many in Shakespeare's audience of the voyage to the Arctic made in 1596–7 by the Dutchman, William Barents. But Fabian cleverly uses it to bring home to Sir Andrew that he can only unfreeze Olivia's iciness towards him by some brave or political action. Sir Andrew instantly chooses valour, and uses another contemporary reference familiar to Elizabethans, saying he would as soon be 'a Brownist as a politician': 'Brownists' were strict puritans who followed the extremist Robert Brown. Sir Toby seizes the opportunity: Sir Andrew must challenge Cesario. Winning the duel will surely win Olivia's love.

Toby instructs Andrew in the fiery terms and insulting detail of the challenge. He should use 'thou' (to give offence, implying Cesario is of lower status than Andrew, a knight), and the paper on which the challenge is written could be as large as 'the bed of Ware in England' (a huge bed for eleven people). Sir Andrew is convinced, and leaves to write it. Just as Malvolio was gulled without difficulty, so too is Sir Andrew. Left alone with Fabian, Sir Toby reveals just what he thinks of Andrew: a man easily cheated out of his money, and a coward.

Maria invites the two men to laugh at the sight of the transformed Malvolio. He has followed the forged letter in every detail and is in yellow stockings and cross-garters. To describe how Malvolio smiles, Maria uses yet another image that would be familiar to the play's first audiences: a map of India and the Far East published in 1599 had lines radiating out from different points like wrinkles around the eyes:

> He does smile his face into more lines than is in the new map
> with the augmentation of the Indies   *(lines 61–3)*

Act 3 Scene 3

So far in Act 3, Shakespeare has whetted the audience's appetite for seeing how the plot complexities will work out: Olivia's misplaced love for Viola, and the practical jokes being played on Sir Andrew and Malvolio. Shakespeare now returns attention to a pair of characters who will add further complications to the inter-related plot tangles: Antonio, driven by his passionate feelings for Sebastian, 'More sharp than filèd steel', has followed him in order to protect him; Sebastian, all too aware he has lost all his possessions in the shipwreck, can reward his friend only with many thanks.

Antonio reveals he is Orsino's enemy, having once fought in a sea-battle against him. Antonio is now a wanted man in Illyria, having refused to repay what he captured in the sea-fight. Now, fearing capture, Antonio declines to join Sebastian in sight-seeing. His fear suggests a darker aspect of Illyria, where enemies of the state are actively sought out for punishment. A few productions have chosen to build this threatening, 'political' aspect of the fairy-tale country into their stagings.

Antonio gives his purse to Sebastian. Like so many other incidents in the play, it is an action that will have its own complicated consequences when the various groups of characters eventually intertwine. But at this moment the evident friendship of the two men stands in contrast to the false or misplaced emotional relationships of other characters in the play. They promise to meet at 'th'Elephant', perhaps a joking reference by Shakespeare to an inn close by his own Globe theatre on London's Bankside.

Act 3 Scene 4

Olivia is looking forward to Viola-Cesario's return, and thinking how she might entertain 'him', and what she might give 'him'. Perhaps somewhat cynically, she reflects that young men are often 'bought' by such gifts. In what seems a change of mood, she sends for Malvolio, feeling that his serious mood and appearance is suitable for her present condition. Maria warns that Malvolio is behaving very strangely, but Olivia sees in that further parallels with her own disturbed emotional state:

> Go call him hither. I am as mad as he
> If sad and merry madness equal be.   *(lines 14–15)*

Malvolio's entrance is an epic moment in every production. Dressed in yellow stockings and cross-garters, he smiles and speaks quite contrary to his usual style: 'Sweet lady, ho, ho!' Olivia, who knows nothing of the forged letter, is astonished by his appearance and behaviour. Her amazement grows as he refers to the letter and quotes from it. Actors playing Malvolio seize every opportunity to exploit the comic potential of his lines: his display of his yellow stockings; his discomfort at the tightness of the cross-gartering; his eager delight as he thinks Olivia invites him to bed; his flirting as he quotes the sentiments he believes Olivia will recognise as her own invitations to him to woo her ('Be not afraid of greatness' and so on). As Malvolio kisses his hands and shows off his yellow stockings, the audience enjoys the absurdity of the situation: the pompous puritanical steward deceived by his own sense of self-importance. Like so much of the play, the disjunction between reality and appearance adds to the comic effect.

Olivia leaves to meet Cesario, but her parting words contribute further to Malvolio's delusion and his imminent downfall:

> Good Maria, let this fellow be looked to. Where's my cousin
> Toby? Let some of my people have a special care of him; I
> would not have him miscarry for the half of my dowry.
>
> *(lines 55–7)*

Malvolio convinces himself that what Olivia has said means that she loves him. He believes that she wishes him, as the letter instructs, to be rude to Sir Toby (in some productions he takes the letter from his pocket and reads the words from it). He interprets her use of 'fellow' as the concluding piece of evidence that he has 'limed her' (caught her in the same way that birds were trapped with glue-like lime spread on branches). Malvolio thanks Jove (the god whose sexual exploits were renowned) as he sees all his hopes finally coming true: marriage to Olivia, and high social status. But the entrance of Sir Toby, Maria and Fabian spells trouble for Malvolio's ludicrously mistaken ambitions.

The three conspirators torment Malvolio. They seize on his every remark to accuse him of being possessed by devils. An Elizabethan audience would quickly recognise Sir Toby's reference to 'Legion' as a quotation from St Mark's Gospel in the Bible, in which Jesus cast out a legion (many thousands) of devils from a madman. Malvolio disdainfully ignores or rejects the taunting, and seems offended by Maria's mock-religious horror, and her advice that he should pray. He stalks out with all the dignity he can muster (difficult in yellow stockings), confident he is of quite different quality from his tormentors. Shakespeare daringly gives Fabian a sentence that always makes the audience laugh as they appreciate that they are indeed watching an improbable fiction. Fabian's 'If' suddenly becomes a deceptive reality:

> If this were played upon a stage now, I could condemn it as an
> improbable fiction.   *(lines 108–9)*

Sir Toby maliciously plans to further humiliate Malvolio. Many Elizabethans believed that a mad person could be cured by imprisoning them in a dark room. Sir Toby proposes to subject Malvolio to this cruel 'cure'. But Malvolio's humiliation must wait until Act 4, because Shakespeare now develops other comic plots. The first concerns Sir Andrew, and Fabian's comment on his entry signals that more holiday humour is to come:

> More matter for a May morning!   *(line 120)*

Sir Andrew has written his challenge to Cesario. His contorted letter reveals that he has taken care to address Cesario by the insulting 'thou' (as Sir Toby had advised him). But it also makes clear that Andrew wishes to ensure that his challenge does not land him in court. Many critics interpret this as Shakespeare writing especially for an audience of law students at the Inns of Court (see page 57). Lawyers would relish the humour in Sir Andrew's evasions.

Sir Toby orders Sir Andrew to challenge Cesario personally in the orchard, but after Andrew has left, Toby reveals what he really thinks: the letter shows Andrew to be a blockhead ('clodpole'). Toby plans to trick both duellists into mutual fright. He will tell each that the other is a superb swordsman, so that they will be terrified of each other. Just as he enjoys gulling Malvolio, so Sir Toby relishes playing a harsh practical joke on his 'friend', manoeuvring him into foolish behaviour (and possibly endangering his life). In both plots, the unattractive side of Sir Toby's character is very evident.

Toby leaves to prepare his own version of the challenge to Cesario, and in the brief episode that follows Olivia once again reveals her passionate love for Viola-Cesario and gives 'him' a jewel. As before, Viola urges her to love Orsino instead, but Olivia is adamant, and in a rhyming couplet as she leaves expresses the emotional torment that her love for Cesario causes her:

> Well, come again tomorrow. Fare thee well.
> A friend like thee might bear my soul to hell.   *(lines 183–4)*

The meeting between Olivia and Viola is short, and recapitulates the nature of their previous encounter. But Shakespeare uses it as a dramatic bridge to continue the comic action, reminding the audience of the absurdity of Olivia's love, and ensuring that Viola will now be drawn into Sir Toby's malicious scheme. The entrapment begins immediately as Toby warns Viola-Cesario to draw 'his' sword and face Sir Andrew's rage and supreme swordsmanship. Toby paints a picture of a furious and formidable opponent, 'bloody as the hunter', who has already killed three men. Viola, probably both puzzled and frightened, tries to avoid the duel, denying she knows anything of the knight who challenges her. First Toby, then Fabian, prevent her leaving, both men adding graphic descriptions of Sir Andrew's bravery and fencing skill.

The humour increases with the entry of the equally frightened Sir Andrew, terrified by Sir Toby's vivid descriptions of Cesario's deadly skill with the sword. Toby adds a detail that would be well known to Shakespeare's first audiences: 'They say he has been fencer to the sophy.' The sophy was the Shah of Persia, and in 1600 Sir Anthony Sherley had published an account of his adventures whilst serving as ambassador to the court of the Shah. Sir Anthony's brother was still serving in the Shah's army during the time of the play's first performances. The exotic image usually evokes a shuddering reaction from Sir Andrew, and he promises to give Sir Toby his horse if he can persuade Viola-Cesario to call off the duel.

The reluctant encounter between Sir Andrew and Viola makes hilariously funny theatre. Both are terrified of each other, and Sir Toby and Fabian do all they can to heighten the fear. Viola's aside, ironic and sexually suggestive, adds to the comedy:

> Pray God defend me! A little thing would make me tell them
> how much I lack of a man.   *(lines 255–6)*

On stage, the mock fight sometimes lasts for several minutes as the terrified opponents, spurred on by Sir Toby and Fabian, ludicrously lunge at each other. In some productions they cover their eyes, afraid to look at each other, and jump back fearfully at any touch of swords. But the entrance of Antonio dramatically changes the mood.

Antonio, seeing Viola (who he takes to be Sebastian), draws his sword and intervenes on her behalf. Sir Toby challenges him, but as the two men prepare to fence, the officers enter and arrest Antonio as Orsino's enemy. Antonio obeys the officers but, continuing to mistake Viola for Sebastian, asks her for the return of his money (which he lent at the end of Act 3 Scene 3). Viola, clearly puzzled, never having seen Antonio before, offers him half of her own small amount of money. Antonio expresses his incredulity and disappointment at the apparent ingratitude, and is further amazed by Viola's denial of knowledge of any kindness he has done her and declaration that she hates ingratitude. He tells how he saved 'This youth' from the shipwreck, and loved and served him. But now 'this god' has proved a vile idol. Naming Sebastian, Antonio reflects that only ill-nature can be called 'deformed', and that good looks can hide bad character. His lines are an eloquent expression of the theme of false appearance:

> In nature there's no blemish but the mind:
> None can be called deformed but the unkind.
> Virtue is beauty, but the beauteous-evil
> Are empty trunks, o'er-flourished by the devil.   *(lines 318–21)*

Grievously disappointed by the apparent betrayal of the beautiful young man he had loved and trusted, Antonio is led away. Viola leaves, hoping that Antonio's mistake means that her brother is still alive, because she is dressed precisely in his fashion. Sir Toby condemns Viola-Cesario for denying 'his' friendship with Antonio, and labels him a coward. Sir Andrew, believing that Cesario really is a coward, vows to follow and beat 'him'. His intention will have unexpectedly violent but comic consequences, even though Sir Toby, always contemptuous of Sir Andrew, expresses scepticism that anything will come of Andrew's new-found courage:

> I dare lay any money, 'twill be nothing yet.   *(line 344)*

Act 3: Critical review

The play's insistence on the instability of language comes into full focus in Act 3 with Feste's opening wordplay and his insistence that he is Olivia's 'corrupter of words'. Just as Viola's disguise causes problems of mistaken identity, so the language of the play makes it easy to turn meaning inside out in Illyria.

The difference between reality and illusion continues to be pervasive, as expressed by Viola (Cesario) in her declaration 'I am not what I am'. Olivia mistakes her for a male. Other characters similarly fail to perceive the truth that lies behind outward show. Sir Andrew cannot see he is mocked and tricked by Sir Toby and Fabian. Malvolio quite mistakes Olivia's response to his ludicrous love overtures. Both Andrew and Viola are deceived by each other's duelling abilities, and Antonio mistakes Viola for Sebastian as he intervenes in the duel.

As Shakespeare begins to weave the three plots in the play together in Act 3 (love, the gulling of Malvolio, Antonio and Sebastian), he creates a growing sense of different kinds of madness. Olivia's passion makes her wrongly believe that Viola's concealed love will surely shine out ('Love's night is noon'). Hearing that Malvolio is 'tainted in's wits' she declares 'I am as mad as he'. She describes Malvolio's strange behaviour as 'very midsummer madness', and Malvolio's tormentors label him as mad, possessed by devils. The entry of Sir Andrew is 'More matter for a May morning!', and the arresting Officer declares of Antonio 'The man grows mad.' Illyria's capacity for inducing mental derangement is evident as Shakespeare richly prepares the ground for the treatment of Malvolio as an actual madman in the following act.

Shakespeare's awareness of theatre underpins the act. Fabian's audience-aware remark 'If this were played upon a stage now, I could condemn it as an improbable fiction' exemplifies what is today called metatheatre: drama that acknowledges its own theatricality. In the duel episode, the situation may seem threatening, but in the theatre the audience's reaction is one of laughter rather than alarm. The audience recognises that the play is a comedy, and the genre guarantees that no real harm will come to Viola.

Act 4 Scene 1

The theme of mistaken identity pervades Scene 1. It begins with Feste wrongly taking Sebastian for Cesario. In response to Sebastian's brusque dismissal, Feste impatiently reveals he has been sent by Olivia to fetch Cesario. His series of negatives (lines 4–7) end with an expression that might well stand for the play itself, in which appearances are so deceptive:

> Nothing that is so is so. *(lines 6–7)*

Feste's words irritate Sebastian further, but Feste mocks the pretension of the order to 'vent thy folly somewhere else'. Sebastian, probably even more irritated, tries to get rid of Feste with money and a threat. He gets no opportunity to respond to yet another of Feste's jibes because Sir Andrew enters and, also mistaking him for Cesario, strikes him. Sebastian, enraged at all this mad treatment by total strangers, beats Sir Andrew again and again. He now finds himself unaccountably challenged by yet another stranger (Sir Toby), and within moments the two men are facing each other, swords drawn, with the prospect of bloodshed imminent.

Sebastian is bewildered. In the space of a few minutes he has met a Fool who calls him Cesario and talks incomprehensibly about an invitation from a lady. Then he is assaulted by one man and challenged to a duel by another. Now something even more hallucinatory happens. A beautiful woman appears, orders his strange tormentors away, then speaks lovingly to him and invites him into her house. He does not know she is Olivia, who, alerted by Feste to the brawl, has also mistaken him for Cesario. Sebastian's response to this new and welcome surprise has echoes of his sister's reaction when she too found herself in a perplexing situation in Act 2 Scene 2. Just as Viola had resolved to let time untangle the complexities of love, so too Sebastian wonders at, but accepts the strange enchantment of it all, and decides to enjoy whatever the experience brings:

> What relish is in this? How runs the stream?
> Or I am mad, or else this is a dream.
> Let fancy still my sense in Lethe steep;
> If it be thus to dream, still let me sleep! *(lines 53–6)*

So decided, Sebastian readily accepts Olivia's eager invitation, 'be ruled by me'. She thinks she has just saved the love of her life, and she now feels that Cesario will accept her love. For the audience, this final moment of the scene, as the two characters glimpse happiness together ahead, can be both funny and moving.

Act 4 Scene 2

Malvolio's tormentors have put their plan into action. Malvolio is imprisoned as a madman, and is about to be subjected to further humiliation. Maria encourages Feste to disguise himself as Sir Topas, the curate. Feste does so, even though it seems unnecessary because Malvolio is unable to see him. Perhaps Shakespeare uses the device as yet another example of mistaken identity, and because at the time priests like Sir Topas were regarded as great scholars but their learning was traditionally the subject of many jokes. Feste immediately exploits that tradition as he parodies the academic style of churchmen with his pretentious language and mock logic. He invents a totally fictitious expert ('the old hermit of Prague') and imitates philosophical talk: 'That that is, is' (a statement that is directly opposite to what he said in the previous scene: 'Nothing that is so is so'). Shakespeare is deepening the sense of the topsy-turvy world of Illyria where appearances are deceptive and all things are possible – or impossible!

Sir Toby had proposed to have Malvolio 'in a dark room and bound'. Every production decides how to stage the imprisonment (Malvolio must be able to hear Feste but not see him). In one staging, he was chained to a stake like a bear; in another, caged like a lion. In a third, only his hands could be seen as they reached through a grill. There have been a multitude of other imaginative settings, but it is vital that whatever staging is used, the audience should understand what is going on. It is probable that Elizabethans more easily accepted the stage convention that Feste is unseen by Malvolio than do today's audiences. For them, no elaborate stage set was necessary.

In his disguise as Sir Topas, Feste begins to torment Malvolio, treating him as if he were mad, possessed by a 'fiend'. Feste's behaviour thus reflects the contemporary belief that mentally-disturbed people were possessed by evil spirits. He calls Malvolio 'lunatic' and 'Satan', deliberately misinterprets his words, suggests he is sexually obsessed, and denies that Malvolio is kept in darkness.

Malvolio repeatedly protests he is not mad, but whatever he says, he cannot win, because Feste is determined to treat all his remarks as though they were made by a madman. Feste's strategy is evident: he will turn logic on its head, claiming darkness is light, speaking nonsense in order to increase Malvolio's confusion and frustration.

Perhaps the most maddening example of Feste's trickery occurs as Malvolio invites 'Sir Topas' to test his sanity. Feste's 'test' concerns Pythagoras, the Greek philosopher and mathematician who in Shakespeare's time was best known for his doctrine of transmigration of souls: that when a person dies, his or her soul migrates to another human or animal body. As a devout Puritan, Malvolio would find Pythagoras' notion very offensive (the doctrine of transmigration was rejected in Christian teaching). But Feste as Sir Topas condemns Malvolio's rejection of Pythagoras' view, and insists he will only judge him sane when he holds a similar view:

> Thou shalt hold th'opinion of Pythagoras ere I will allow of thy wits, and fear to kill a woodcock lest thou dispossess the soul of thy grandam. *(lines 44–6)*

Sir Toby, knowing he is increasingly in disfavour with Olivia, wishes the whole business ('sport') of tormenting Malvolio was over, and leaves, ordering Maria to come shortly to his bedroom. He seems motivated more by regard for his own position in Olivia's household than by any compassion for Malvolio.

Feste sings in his own voice, and Malvolio begs him to bring pen and paper so that he may write a letter to Olivia. Feste continues the tormenting. He pretends not to hear, then seizes on Malvolio's claim to be as sane as he is: 'Then you are mad indeed, if you be no better in your wits than a fool.' The malicious teasing continues as Feste pretends to have a conversation with Sir Topas (adding yet another layer to the theme of mistaken identity). Malvolio, increasingly desperate, pleads again for pen, ink and paper to write his letter. At last, perhaps feeling he has at last got his own back for how Malvolio humiliated him in the first act, Feste agrees to do as Malvolio wishes, but the song he sings as he leaves, with its mention of the comic villain Vice from medieval morality plays, contains more mocking nonsense. He may even direct the final line to the sorely distressed Malvolio:

Adieu, goodman devil. *(line 113)*

The whole scene poses crucial questions for each new production of the play. Should Feste display open malice in his tormenting? What degree of audience sympathy for Malvolio should the performance attempt to evoke? What kind of humour is in the scene? What kind of audience laughter is sought in performance? Does Malvolio deserve what he gets? Different valid answers can be given to each of these questions, but it seems likely that in Shakespeare's time audience reaction to Malvolio's plight was much less sympathetic than it is today, and the laughter less affected by doubt as to its appropriateness (see pages 67, 83).

Act 4 Scene 3

After the tormenting of Malvolio, the scene changes to Sebastian wondering at his good fortune. The claustrophobia of the dark room gives way to fresh air and sunshine. The theme of madness connects the two scenes, but in contrast to the false accusations levelled at Malvolio, Sebastian decides that the strange events that have happened to him are not due to madness:

> This is the air, that is the glorious sun,
> This pearl she gave me, I do feel't and see't,
> And though 'tis wonder that enwraps me thus,
> Yet 'tis not madness. *(lines 1–4)*

Sebastian is puzzled by what has happened to Antonio, whose advice he needs to help him understand his bewildering but fortunate situation. He feels ready to distrust the evidence of his eyes, but resolves (just as Malvolio had done in the previous scene) that he is not mad. Neither is Olivia, because she rules her household with total competence. The conclusion of his soliloquy provides yet another description of the unreliability of appearances in Illyria:

> There's something in't
> That is deceivable. *(lines 20–1)*

Olivia's entry with a Priest brings more wonder for Sebastian. She still believes he is Cesario, and proposes an instant marriage, but to keep it secret until Sebastian is willing to make it public. When that time comes, they will have a grand ceremony ('celebration'), suitable for her high social status ('birth'). Sebastian's assent and Olivia's final command and hope for the future have a fairy-tale quality about them, caught in the chiming formality and 'happy ever after' spirit of the final couplets as they leave to be married by the Priest:

SEBASTIAN   I'll follow this good man, and go with you,
    And having sworn truth, ever will be true.
OLIVIA   Then lead the way, good father, and heavens so shine,
    That they may fairly note this act of mine!

(lines 32–5)

Act 4: Critical review

Act 4, like the preceding acts, is much concerned with how identities come to be mistaken as characters fail to see beyond mere appearances. Feste, Sir Andrew and Sir Toby mistake Sebastian for Cesario, with violent results for the two knights. Olivia makes a similar mistake, but this time with a happy outcome in Scene 3 as she prepares their marriage. In Scene 2 the imprisoned Malvolio is deceived into thinking that Feste is Sir Topas and will help him.

Scene 2 can be seen today to present a crucial test of audience response. It shows the heartless tormenting of the imprisoned Malvolio, and is often claimed to highlight an essential difference between Shakespeare's times and our own. The argument goes that Elizabethans were fascinated by madness, and enjoyed visiting asylums where mentally disturbed people were kept. It was a kind of sport to watch their antics and hear their strange language. Today such attitudes and practices are viewed with abhorrence, because sympathetic compassion has replaced the cruel voyeurism that found fun in displays of madness. Audience response today is therefore likely to be very complicated. Audiences can still find humour in the scene, but they often also experience ambivalence, or even revulsion, at the malicious way in which Malvolio is taunted and humiliated.

For the watching audience, there is a similar puzzle about how to respond to the improbabilities of Scene 3 as Olivia prepares to marry the bewildered but contented Sebastian. Because Shakespeare has ensured that the audience by now is accustomed to the uncertainty of anything to do with Illyria, there is no point in asking obvious practical questions: Why does she not call Sebastian 'Cesario' and so discover her mistake? What happened in the house between Sebastian and Olivia? Such questions are unimportant. Illyria is a fictional world of playful imagination; a dramatic construct, not reality. Nonetheless, Scene 3 reveals Shakespeare's further dramatic exploration of the madness that results from love and illusion. Sebastian persuades himself that the unreal experience he is caught up in, for all that it is 'deceivable' cannot be madness. Yet Olivia is led by her eyes alone as she fails to see that the man she is about to marry is not the young page of Orsino's with whom she fell in love.

Act 5 Scene 1

The act begins with Feste refusing to let Fabian see the letter that Malvolio has written to Olivia:

FABIAN   Now, as thou lov'st me, let me see his letter.
FESTE   Good Master Fabian, grant me another request.
FABIAN   Anything.
FESTE   Do not desire to see this letter.
FABIAN   This is to give a dog and in recompense desire my dog
      again.   *(lines 1–5)*

Today, every audience can appreciate the witty way in which Feste deflects Fabian's request, but Elizabethan audiences would laugh at Fabian's response (line 5) because of a well-known story of the time. Queen Elizabeth begged a dog from a courtier, saying she would grant any request in return. He replied, 'Give me my dog again.' There is another contemporary reference in Feste's subsequent word-juggling that entertains Orsino ('your four negatives make your two affirmatives'): a favourite joke among men at the time was that a girl's 'no, no, no, no' meant 'yes, yes'. Similarly, Feste refers to the triple peal of the bells of St Bennet, a London church. Such knowledge, familiar to Elizabethans, is unknown to most people today, but the general sense of the lines can be understood, and their amusing quality can be conveyed by Feste's fluent delivery.

Orsino has come to Olivia's house to see her himself. (He is also probably wondering what has happened to his messenger, Cesario.) Duke Orsino is the most powerful person in Illyria, and he seems to enjoy Feste's witticisms and begging for money. But on stage, Feste's dialogue with Orsino can be played with mockery or even disrespect. In a few productions in which Feste has been played that way, Orsino has shown he suspects he is being mocked, speaking his lines with increasing irritation. But however the exchange is played, the episode ends with Feste leaving at Orsino's command to fetch Olivia.

As Feste exits, Antonio is brought in by the officers. Viola recognises him as the stranger who rescued her from the duel, and Orsino and the First Officer reveal just who he is. Their stories explain that Antonio is a wanted man in Illyria because he performed great deeds in a destructive fight against Orsino's fleet. Antonio's own tiny, almost valueless ship outfought Orsino's best vessel and captured another with all her cargo from Crete ('the Phoenix and her fraught from Candy'). He boarded another of Orsino's ships, the Tiger, and in the battle Orsino's nephew Titus lost his leg. Even though Antonio inflicted terrible losses on his Illyrian enemies, Orsino admits that his bravery won their admiration:

> That very envy, and the tongue of loss,
> Cried fame and honour on him. *(lines 47–8)*

Up to this moment in the play, Orsino has appeared as the romantic besotted lover, concerned only with his personal emotions. Now he takes on his official duty as head of state, and speaks in high heroic style ('As black as Vulcan, in the smoke of war') as military commander and ruler. His condemnation of Antonio is harsh:

> Notable pirate! Thou salt-water thief! *(line 58)*

Antonio denies he is a pirate or thief. As he explains why he voluntarily risked the danger of returning to a country where he was actively sought as an enemy, the plot returns from its momentary social focus on affairs of state to the personal and emotional concerns of the play and its preoccupation with mistaken identity. Antonio is firmly convinced that Viola is Sebastian. He tells how he rescued Sebastian, served him, lent him money, and protected him in the threatened duel. Now Sebastian, out of deceit and cowardice, denies their friendship, and has become coldly distant:

> his false cunning
> (Not meaning to partake with me in danger)
> Taught him to face me out of his acquaintance,
> And grew a twenty-years' removèd thing
> While one would wink *(lines 75–9)*

Throughout Antonio's story Viola usually shows increasing perplexity, expressed finally in her 'How can this be?' But it seems equally likely that as she listens she also experiences dawning hope that her brother may be alive. When Antonio reveals he has kept company with Sebastian for three months, Orsino dismisses his story as madness, because Viola-Cesario has been in his service for three months (in some productions Orsino here clearly reveals puzzlement about his page's ambiguous nature). Theatre audiences rarely notice that at this point Shakespeare seems to have forgotten what he wrote earlier in the play when (in Act 1 Scene 4, lines 2–3) Valentine said that Orsino has known Viola 'but three days'. However, such a discrepancy does not matter in a play set in the bewildering world of Illyria, and Antonio is ordered aside as Olivia and her attendants enter, greeted with Orsino's soaring praise:

Here comes the countess; now heaven walks on earth.

(line 86)

This is the first time that Orsino and Olivia have met in the play, and every staging strives to bring out through their actions and expressions just how they feel for each other. Orsino's attention is wholly on Olivia, but she seems merely polite to him. Her concern is only for Viola-Cesario. She mistakes 'him' for Sebastian, whom she has married only two hours before. What is her bridegroom doing back in the service of the Duke? Olivia accuses Viola-Cesario of not keeping 'his' promise to her, then again dismisses Orsino's love.

Orsino reacts vehemently at this ungrateful rejection of his religious-like devotion to her. Uncertain what to do, but spurred by her indifference, Orsino displays a cruel streak. He first threatens to kill Olivia out of 'savage jealousy' (as did 'th'Egyptian thief' of legend). He then threatens to kill Viola-Cesario, revealing he suspects 'him' of having stolen Olivia's affections. He orders Viola to follow him, and with an ominous religious metaphor proposes to kill 'him' to spite Olivia. Viola's willing compliance shows the extremity of her love for Orsino:

ORSINO   I'll sacrifice the lamb that I do love,
        To spite a raven's heart within a dove.
VIOLA   And I most jocund, apt, and willingly,
        To do you rest, a thousand deaths would die.   *(lines 119–22)*

As Viola declares her love for Orsino, Olivia feels she has been deceived. She sends for the Priest, and calls after the departing Viola. Her cry makes an arresting moment of theatre, amazing everyone on stage, freezing all action, and holding the audience in suspense, on the brink of laughter, but holding its breath to see what will happen to this open revelation of mistaken identity:

> Cesario, husband, stay! *(line 132)*

Orsino's response (often after a long silence-filled pause) is to repeat that single unbelievable word:

> Husband? *(line 133)*

Viola can only deny the allegation, but Olivia urges 'him' not to be afraid, but to admit what 'he' truly is. Her words challenge the notion of false identity: 'Be that thou know'st thou art'. Increasing the amazement of everyone on stage, the Priest confirms that the marriage took place only two hours ago. The revelation provokes Orsino to harsh condemnation of Viola as he wonders what one so young and so false will become as he grows to grey-haired maturity:

> O thou dissembling cub! What wilt thou be
> When time hath sowed a grizzle on thy case? *(lines 153–4)*

Orsino orders Viola away with Olivia, vowing never to meet 'him' again. At this moment every character on stage is bemused and astonished, but Shakespeare now changes the mood again and further compounds dramatic complexity. Sir Andrew enters, his head bleeding, and complaining that he and Sir Toby have been violently assaulted by Cesario:

> For the love of God, a surgeon! *(line 161)*

Andrew usually evokes audience sympathy as he declares plaintively 'I had rather than forty pound I were at home.' It is a touching moment, rather like his earlier wistful recollection 'I was adored once, too.' But the moment passes, and in performance there is often a hilarious moment as Sir Andrew does a fearful and incredulous double-take as he catches sight of Viola, who he thinks has beaten him: 'Od's lifelings, here he is!' Viola, once again the victim of mistaken identity, denies doing any harm, but Sir Andrew persists with his accusation and says that Sir Toby, entering drunk and similarly bloodied, will confirm the charge. Sir Toby, however, has no time or sympathy for Andrew. He calls for a doctor, but hearing from Feste that the doctor is also drunk, calls him 'a rogue, and a passy-measures pavin'. Toby's phrase has baffled all critics, but it may possibly mean 'drunken slowcoach' (Sir Toby's slurred speaking of 'passing measure pavane' – a slow and stately dance).

This final appearance of Toby and Andrew shows more of the sour aspect of Toby's character, and offers only more humiliation for Andrew. Sir Toby drops his mask of friendship with Andrew and contemptuously rejects his offer of help. He snarls only a cruel dismissal of the foolish knight whom he has robbed and tricked:

> Will you help – an ass-head, and a coxcomb, and a knave, a
> thin-faced knave, a gull?   *(lines 190–1)*

Shakespeare provides yet other dramatic surprise as he varies the mood yet again with the entry of Sebastian. Once again everyone on stage is amazed, this time by the sight of Viola-Cesario's double. In the stunned silence, as Sebastian apologises to Olivia for hurting Sir Toby, he recognises her astonishment: 'You throw a strange regard upon me'. Orsino, looking from Viola to Sebastian, and from Sebastian to Viola, speaks for everyone:

> One face, one voice, one habit, and two persons –
> A natural perspective, that is and is not!   *(lines 200–1)*

Orsino's words are apt. 'A natural perspective' is a distorting mirror that makes one image into two, and 'that is and is not' could well be the motto of Illyria, a place of seemingly impossible happenings. More amazement follows. Sebastian greets Antonio with intense relief at finding him. Antonio speaks the question that is in everyone's mind as they feel unable to believe the evidence of their own eyes:

> How have you made division of yourself?
> An apple cleft in two is not more twin
> Than these two creatures.   *(lines 206–8)*

Olivia's response invariably evokes audience laughter as she contemplates the vision of two husbands:

Most wonderful! *(line 209)*

Sebastian, prompted by Antonio's and Olivia's words and actions (they look in wonder from twin to twin) at last catches sight of Viola. The emotional atmosphere changes yet again as both begin to realise that they might indeed be about to find their twin whom they feared they had lost for ever. Both are near to tears, and their exchanges are tentative and cautious, a mixture of fear and hope for the miracle of family reunion. Sebastian poignantly puts that hope into words:

> Were you a woman – as the rest goes even –
> I should my tears let fall upon your cheek,
> And say, 'Thrice welcome, drownèd Viola.' *(lines 223–5)*

It is the first time that Viola's name has been spoken in the play, and it signals the change from hope to joyous certainty as brother and sister discover they both come from Messaline, have a father's name in common, and each lost their twin in a shipwreck. The confirming domestic details continue: the mole on their father's neck, his death when Viola was 13. Viola tells of her disguise and of the Captain who helped her gain employment with Orsino. At last Viola and Sebastian are reunited, and their mutual rediscovery can be an intensely moving theatrical experience.

The consequences of the discovery unfold, once more creating shifting moods. Sebastian's comment that Olivia was betrothed to 'a maid' usually evokes audience laughter, but his admission that he himself is a virgin ('maid and man') can create a quiet moment of admiring respect for Sebastian's integrity. Similarly, Orsino's quick determination to 'share in this most happy wreck' also raises laughter which modulates into the satisfaction of hearing Viola confirm her absolute love for him in a soaring image of the constancy of the sun:

> And all those sayings will I overswear,
> And all those swearings keep as true in soul
> As doth that orbèd continent the fire
> That severs day from night. *(lines 253–6)*

Shakespeare uses the mutual declaration of love by Viola and Orsino as a dramatic bridge to bring Malvolio back into the play. Orsino wishes to see Viola in her woman's clothes, but Viola tells him that the Captain who rescued her has her clothing, and he has been arrested on the order of Malvolio. Just why Malvolio has had the Captain imprisoned is never made clear, but it may provide yet another clue to his intimidating character, always seeking to control others. Olivia orders the Captain's release and sends for Malvolio. She recalls his bizarre behaviour, and finds in it an echo of her own:

> They say, poor gentleman, he's much distract.
> A most extracting frenzy of mine own
> From my remembrance clearly banished his.   *(lines 264–6)*

The stage is set for Malvolio's entry, but first Shakespeare has his distressed condition reported by Feste: 'he holds Belzebub at the stave's end' (he is fighting to keep the devil at a distance). Feste begins to read Malvolio's letter madly, but Olivia stops him and orders Fabian to read. The letter complains that Olivia has done Malvolio wrong, and reports his suffering at the hands of Sir Toby, and his indignation at his treatment. It ends with his description of himself as 'The madly used Malvolio.'

Olivia again orders Malvolio to be brought in, and in the brief time before he appears she proposes joint wedding celebrations for the two couples at her house. Orsino agrees, and offers his hand in marriage to Viola. She makes no reply, and indeed does not speak again in the play, but virtually all performances and criticism interpret her responding positively. The mood is warm and loving, but it chills and becomes threatening with the entry of Malvolio and his accusation of Olivia:

> Madam, you have done me wrong,
> Notorious wrong.   *(lines 307–8)*

Malvolio may still be wearing the absurd clothes he had worn to woo Olivia. On stage he has often appeared dishevelled and besmirched, sometimes in pyjamas, rags, or a straitjacket. But whatever his costume, he usually behaves with exaggerated calm and controlled dignity, speaking in verse for the first time in the play. He shows Olivia the forged letter and demands an explanation of why she hinted she loved him, told him to appear smiling and in yellow stockings and cross-gartered, and caused him to be imprisoned in a dark house, humiliated and tricked. Why has she behaved so abominably? His 'why?' is three times repeated.

Olivia recognises that the letter is a forgery by Maria. She sympathetically acknowledges that Malvolio has been duped, and offers him justice: he can be both accuser and judge of his own case. Fabian, probably worried about how his own part in the trickery will affect his position in Olivia's household, gives a full explanation. He and Toby set up the plot out of dislike of Malvolio; Toby persuaded Maria to write the letter, and to reward her has married her. Fabian hopes that laughter rather than revenge will be the outcome. Olivia expresses sympathy for Malvolio:

Alas, poor fool, how have they baffled thee!   (line 348)

Malvolio has to suffer further embarrassment at the hands of Feste, who quotes tauntingly from the letter, reveals that he was Sir Topas, and reminds Malvolio of his sneering dismissal of him on his first appearance (Act 1 Scene 5, lines 67–71). Feste relishes how time has brought Malvolio low:

And thus the whirligig of time brings in his revenges.

(lines 353–4)

How does Malvolio behave throughout this long exposure of his folly at falling for a trick that appealed to his sense of self-importance? Both the theatre audience and the on-stage audience have witnessed his shaming, so his emotions are surely immensely powerful, even if he suppresses them. Every production produces its own solution, and decides how he will speak his final unforgiving line:

I'll be revenged on the whole pack of you!   (line 355)

Does Malvolio mean it, or is it only an empty threat like one spoken by an angry impotent child? On stage, the effect of Malvolio's line is often a long silence. In the theatre audience, each person decides whether they feel sympathy for Malvolio as the victim of a cruel hoax, or laugh at him, thinking he has got what he deserves.

Olivia again expresses sympathy: 'He hath been most notoriously abused.' In one production, clearly angry with Feste, she struck him as she spoke the line. Most productions however do not portray this sharp side of Olivia's character, and performances end in a mood of harmony as Orsino sends after Malvolio, hoping to make peace, and looks forward to a 'golden time' of marriage. His final words are to Viola, still dressed as Cesario, hoping to see her in her woman's clothes:

> when in other habits you are seen,
> Orsino's mistress, and his fancy's queen. *(lines 364–5)*

The stage empties of all characters but Feste. Often Antonio is the final character to leave, signifying his 'outsider' status. He has lost Sebastian, and is excluded from the happy future that marriage promises the four main characters. But however the departures are staged, at last only Feste remains. He too is an outsider, nominally a member of Olivia's household, but free to roam in Illyria, strangely independent, and sceptical of all he sees.

Feste's mysterious song is about growing up, being tolerated in childhood, rejected in adulthood, unsuccessful in marriage, and drunk in old age. In its final acknowledgement of the theatricality, not reality, of what the audience has watched, it seems to conclude that nothing really matters, the actors will always try to please:

> A great while ago the world begun,
> With hey, ho, the wind and the rain,
> But that's all one, our play is done,
> And we'll strive to please you every day. *(lines 382–5)*

Act 5: Critical review

Act 5 is one long scene, full of ever-changing moods as it brings together the varied plots and characters of the play. Traditionally, it is critically regarded as true to the genre of comedy: a denouement which humorously resolves the many paradoxes of mistaken identity, reunites the twins, and promises happy marriages ahead.

The illusions that have beset characters are stripped away. In the comic plot Malvolio finds out how he has been tricked, and Sir Andrew learns what Sir Toby really thinks of him. In the love plot Orsino turns from self-indulgent illusion to discover genuine affection for Viola. Olivia at last realises she has been deceived by outward appearances, and finds true love with Sebastian.

But Shakespeare complicates traditional interpretations that the play ends with justice done to Malvolio and with happiness and harmony for the other characters. As Toby and Andrew limp off, all pretence of friendship shattered, audiences today often watch in shocked silence. Shakespeare extinguishes good humour and laughter in revealing Sir Toby's callous disregard for his companion.

Malvolio's threat of revenge prompts similarly troubled responses. Some critics think it foreshadows the English Civil War that began in 1642, just over 40 years after *Twelfth Night* was written. The puritans seized power, executed the king, closed the theatres, and attempted to end all public frivolity and merriment. If that interpretation is true, it shows remarkable prescience on Shakespeare's part. It seems more reasonable to argue that the play explores puritan prejudices against enjoyment, and that this final episode casts a cloud over the joys of the twins' reunion and the prospect of the forthcoming marriages.

The play ends, as it began, with music. Today Feste's song is often seen as creating a sad mood. But when the play was performed in Shakespeare's time, Feste probably danced a jig, and sang in a cheerful manner. Critics have described the song in very different ways, as 'moving and poignant', 'sardonic and satirical', 'melancholy and disturbing'. Such various interpretations display the aptness of *Twelfth Night*'s subtitle *What You Will* with its invitation to each member of the audience to make of the play whatever they wish.

Contexts

The hugely enjoyable film *Shakespeare in Love* portrays a popular belief about the source of Shakespeare's creativity. It shows him suffering from 'writer's block', unable to put pen to paper, with no idea of how to write his next play. But all is resolved when he meets a beautiful young girl (called Viola). His love for her sparks an overwhelming flow of creative energy – and he writes *Romeo and Juliet*!

It is an attractive idea, and the film presents it delightfully (and even ends with Viola alone on a beach and with Shakespeare about to write *Twelfth Night*), but the truth of the matter is far more complex. Like every other writer, Shakespeare was influenced by many factors other than his own personal experience. The society of his time, its practices, beliefs and language in political and economic affairs, culture and religion, were the raw materials on which his imagination worked.

This section identifies the contexts from which *Twelfth Night* emerged: the wide range of different influences which fostered the creativity of Shakespeare as he wrote the play. These contexts ensured that Twelfth Night is full of all kinds of reminders of everyday life, and the familiar knowledge, assumptions, beliefs and values of Elizabethan England.

Before discussing such contexts, it is helpful to note a well-known claim about how *Twelfth Night* came to be written. Although there is a theory that the play was first performed to an audience of law students at one of London's Inns of Court, a much more closely argued assertion is made by Leslie Hotson. He claims that Shakespeare wrote the play in about two weeks for a performance at the court of Queen Elizabeth on Twelfth Night, 1601. Hotson argues that Olivia is a portrayal of Queen Elizabeth, and that the play is a compliment to an Italian nobleman, the Duke of Bracciano, Don Virginio Orsino, who was currently being entertained by the Queen.

Hotson's assertion has been strongly disputed by other critics. They argue that it seems unlikely that Duke Orsino would enjoy seeing himself as Orsino in the play: an ineffectual lover given to self-dramatising verse. Further, Queen Elizabeth would be offended by the suggestion that she was like Olivia: a woman unable to see through disguise. There is also a question of evidence: although Shakespeare's company, The Lord Chamberlain's Men, were playing at court on that day, there is no reliable record of the play they actually performed. However, it is possible that because Duke Orsino's visit to Elizabeth was the subject of much popular gossip, the name may have stuck in Shakespeare's mind and he thought it suitable for his love-struck Illyrian ruler. But like many such possibilities, that is all it can be: a speculation.

What did Shakespeare write?

Sometime during 1600 and 1601 William Shakespeare, already well known as a successful playwright, wrote *Twelfth Night*. The dates are certain for two reasons. First, because Maria's comment about 'the new map with the augmentation of the Indies' (Act 3 Scene 2, lines 62–3) refers to a map of India and the Far East published in 1599. Second, because the first record of a performance of the play is on 2 February 1602. John Manningham, a lawyer, wrote about a performance he saw at the Middle Temple, one of London's Inns of Court. His diary entry reads:

> At our feast we had a play called 'Twelve Night, or What You Will', much like the Comedy of Errors, or Menaechmi in Plautus, but most like and near to that in Italian called Inganni. A good practice in it to make the Steward believe his Lady widow was in love with him, by counterfeiting a letter as from his Lady in general terms, telling him what she liked best in him, and prescribing his gesture in smiling, his apparel, etc., and then when he came to practise making him believe they took him to be mad.

What was the play that Shakespeare wrote and his audiences heard? No one knows for certain because his original script has not survived, nor have any handwritten amendments he might subsequently have made. So what is the origin of the text of the play you are studying? *Twelfth Night* was not published during Shakespeare's lifetime but appeared for the first time in 1623, seven years after his death. It was published in the volume known as the First Folio (a collection of 36 of his plays).

Today, all editions of *Twelfth Night* are based on that 1623 version.

But the edition of the play you are using will vary in many minor respects from other editions. That is because although every editor of the play uses the Folio version, each one makes a multitude of different judgements about such matters as spelling, punctuation, stage directions (entrances and exits, asides, etc.), scene locations and other features. For example, in the 1623 First Folio, Orsino's and Feste's lines have the speech headings (names of speakers) of Du. (Duke) and Clo. (Clown). Today most editions use Orsino and Feste.

So the text of *Twelfth Night* is not as stable as you might think. This is no reason for dismay, but rather an opportunity to think about how the differences reflect what actually happens in performance. Every production, on stage or film, cuts, adapts and amends the text to present its own unique version of *Twelfth Night*. This Guide follows the New Cambridge edition of the play (also used in Cambridge School Shakespeare).

What did Shakespeare read?

Shakespeare's genius lay in his ability to transform what he read into gripping drama. This section is therefore about the influence of genre: the literary contexts of *Twelfth Night*. It identifies the stories and dramatic conventions that fired Shakespeare's imagination as he wrote *Twelfth Night*.

As noted above, John Manningham in 1602 remarked that *Twelfth Night* resembled *Menaechmi* by Plautus, but was 'most like' an Italian play called *Inganni*. The first reference is to a play about twins, and the complications that arise when they are mistaken for each other. The second refers to an Italian play (of which there were several versions), first performed in 1531, *Gl'Ingannati* (The Deceived) in which a woman disguised as a man woos another woman on behalf of the man she really loves. In one version the woman is called Cesare; in another, Fabio.

Shakespeare may or may not have seen productions of these source plays. What seems more certain is that he knew prose versions of their plots. These prose tales existed in Italian (written by Bandello) and in French (by Belleforest). But it seems most likely that Shakespeare found his version of them in a collection of 'histories' written in English: *Barnaby Riche's Farewell to Military Profession*, first published in 1581. There he read a 'historie' *Apolonius and Silla*, which, as the following brief account shows, strongly influenced him as he wrote *Twelfth Night*:

> A duke loves a beautiful young woman. She is dressed in black, mourning her husband. The duke is loved by another young woman who undertakes a sea-voyage, is almost raped by the ship's captain, and is shipwrecked. She disguises herself as a boy, adopts the name of her twin brother, enters the service of the duke as a page, and is sent by him to woo the widow who falls in love with her. Her twin brother arrives, searching for his sister. But he meets the widow, who invites him to spend the night with her. He does so, and the widow becomes pregnant. The next morning the brother leaves, knowing the widow has mistaken his identity.

> The duke suspects his page has deceived him, and imprisons her in a dungeon. The widow claims the page is father of her child, further enraging the duke. The page reveals her true sexual identity, the duke loves and marries her, her twin brother returns and marries the widow. All ends happily with the two weddings.

Major features of *Twelfth Night* are immediately evident in this brief account of *Apolonius and Silla*: shipwreck, twins separated and reunited, disguise, mistaken identity and confusions of love. Evident too are Shakespeare's changes as he avoided the coarseness of his source. The Captain becomes a benign helper, Olivia does not become pregnant, Viola is not imprisoned. More striking is what Shakespeare added to create the dramatic structure of *Twelfth Night*: the comic subplot with the invention of Sir Toby, Sir Andrew, Maria, Feste and Malvolio. But even those characters and situations can be shown to have their origins in Shakespeare's imaginative reworking of literary and real life aspects of his times.

Twelfth Night can also be considered in the context of Shakespeare's writing career. He had explored a number of its elements in two earlier plays, written at least five or six years earlier than *Twelfth Night*: *The Two Gentlemen of Verona* and *The Comedy of Errors*.

In *The Two Gentlemen of Verona* Shakespeare used the plot device of a young woman who, like Viola, disguises herself as a boy (called

Sebastian) to enter the service of the man she loves. He, like Orsino, sends her with messages to woo another woman. In the earlier play, this dramatic action is only a short episode towards the end of the play. However, in *Twelfth Night* it becomes a central part of the plot from Act I, and its emotional potentialities are intensively explored as Viola's disguise has all kinds of unexpected comic and dramatic consequences.

In *The Comedy of Errors* Shakespeare had portrayed not one pair, but two pairs of identical twins separated by a shipwreck. The multiple hilarious confusions of mistaken identity which arise as the separated twins come together in the same town, were almost certainly in his mind as he wrote *Twelfth Night*. In *The Comedy of Errors*, even the wife of one twin mistakes the other for her husband, just as Olivia mistakes Sebastian for Viola. But *Twelfth Night* moves far beyond *The Comedy of Errors* by dramatising in far greater depth the complexity of characters' feelings that arise from mistaken identity. It shows how emotional confusions are resolved, not by accident, as in the earlier play, but by characters' growth of insight into their own and others' feelings.

It is possible that *The Merchant of Venice* may also have been in Shakespeare's mind as he invented the character of Antonio. Like his namesake in *The Merchant*, *Twelfth Night*'s Antonio lends money to a young friend, as a result of which his life is threatened. At the end of both plays, each Antonio seems isolated and unfulfilled, as the young man for whom he risked his life finds happiness in marriage. It can also be noted that some critics have identified parallels between Sir Toby Belch and Falstaff of *King Henry IV Parts 1 and 2*. Both men are disreputable knights who enjoy drinking and festivity, and who exploit other characters. Such parallels can be extended to other characters (see Feste pages 66 and 123, Orsino page 120), but what is more significant is the distinctiveness that Shakespeare gives to each within the dramatic world of *Twelfth Night*.

What was Shakespeare's England like?

Like all writers, Shakespeare reflected in his plays the world he knew. His audiences, watching performances of *Twelfth Night*, would recognise aspects of their own time and country. Make-believe Illyria might sound a faraway place, but *Twelfth Night* is full of the customs, sights and sounds of Elizabethan England.

When Orsino says of Olivia 'Methought she purged the air of pestilence' and when Olivia, feeling she has fallen in love with Cesario, says 'Even so quickly may one catch the plague?', both images are drawn from the everyday experience of Shakespeare's contemporaries. For all Londoners the plague was a constant threat. Almost every member of the audience watching the play would have been affected in some way by the plague. They would know some friend, neighbour, or family member who had fallen victim to the epidemics which occurred frequently in England, and disrupted normal life.

Characters mention place names familiar to contemporary audiences: 'the south suburbs', 'th'Elephant', the chiming bells of St Bennet, the great 'bed of Ware'. Features of everyday Elizabethan life recur in all kinds of ways. Characters refer to such games as tray-trip (dice), cherry-pit (a children's game), bowls, and spinning the parish top. The cruel 'sport' of bear-baiting provides both action and images: Fabian is out of favour with Olivia for arranging a bear-baiting, and Olivia chides Viola in an image of a bear chained to a stake, and attacked by unmuzzled dogs:

> Have you not set mine honour at the stake,
> And baited it with all th'unmuzzled thoughts
> That tyrannous heart can think?

(Act 3 Scene 1, lines 103–5)

Many aspects of everyday life in the Elizabethan world are quietly incorporated into the play. Viola stands like 'a sheriff's post' at Olivia's door; her talk of building a 'willow cabin' at Olivia's gate uses the image conventional at the time of the willow as an emblem of sorrowful love. When Feste (possibly putting his arms around the shoulders of Sir Toby and Sir Andrew) says 'Did you never see the picture of "We Three"?' playgoers would recall the popular inn sign of two fools, which invited the viewer to become the third fool. The intense male friendship of Antonio and Sebastian was customary among Elizabethan men, and caused little comment.

Phrases in the play echo common sayings of the time. Many theatre-goers, waiting to cross the Thames by ferry to the Globe, would hear the ferrymen calling 'Westward ho!' to advertise they were ready to take passengers to Westminster. During the performance they would hear Viola use the expression to declare her intention to leave Olivia. Similarly, the sayings 'It's all one', and 'What you will' were conventional phrases to accompany a shrug of the shoulders.

Everyday Elizabethan knowledge to do with eating and drinking is frequently invoked, assuming the audience's easy familiarity with such things as 'th'buttery-bar', 'canary', 'sack', 'alehouse', and 'tosspots'. Food provides some in-jokes that appealed to contemporary audiences. Sir Toby blames 'pickle herring' as the cause of his belching; Sir Andrew claims that being 'a great eater of beef' resulted in stupidity; and Feste jokes that 'fools are as like husbands as pilchards are to herrings – the husband's the bigger'.

The Elizabethans' enjoyment of songs and dances is also evident in the play. Shakespeare assumed his audiences were well acquainted with different types of dance: jig, galliard, coranto, sink-a-pace (cinquepace), and how to 'cut a caper', or perform a 'back-trick'. Similarly, songs and music unfamiliar to today's audiences were well known to Elizabethans: the 'catch' the revellers sing in Act 2 Scene 3, Viola's mention of 'cantons of contemnèd love', and snatches from contemporary songs sung by Sir Toby and Feste as they bait Malvolio.

A strong sense of Elizabethan England is palpable throughout the play. All kinds of occupations are mentioned: coziers, tinkers, weavers, spinsters (who spin flax on a distaff), knitters, grand jurymen, a bumbailey, a master crowner (coroner), parson, curate, Dick Surgeon, coistrell, groom. Customary features of rural England recur. Olivia's orchard and her garden with the box-tree recall features of well-to-do Elizabethan country homes. Malvolio uses the image of an unripe peapod or apple to describe Cesario: 'as a squash is before 'tis a peascod, or a codling when 'tis almost an apple'. Malvolio is compared to a swelling turkey-cock, Sir Toby remarks scornfully that Sir Andrew has 'dormouse valour', and that 'oxen and wainropes' cannot draw Andrew and Cesario together to fight.

The Elizabethan passion for hunting and field sports pervades *Twelfth Night*, providing striking imagery. In the very first scene, Curio invites Orsino to hunt, and the love-struck Duke seizes the opportunity to picture himself as a hart pursued by 'fell and cruel hounds'. The gulling of Malvolio is rich in such images of animal entrapment. As Malvolio approaches the spot where he will find the forged letter that will so ludicrously ensnare him, Maria uses an image of how fish were caught by stroking: 'here comes the trout that must be caught by tickling'. When Malvolio suddenly catches sight of the letter, Sir Toby's image reflects how wild birds were caught in traps ('gins'): 'Now is the woodcock near the gin.'

During the episode in which Malvolio puzzles his way through the letter, Sir Toby and Fabian use images from Elizabethan field sports to describe what they see. Maria's letter becomes a 'dish o'poison', Malvolio's attempt to find meaning is likened to a kestrel mistakenly flying at prey: 'And with what a wing the staniel checks at it!' When Malvolio fails to make sense of the letters M.O.A.I. (Elizabethans enjoyed such word games and acrostic puzzles), he is first likened to a hound who has lost the trail of a fox: 'He is now at a cold scent', then to a barking hound 'Sowter will cry upon't'. As Malvolio begins to link 'M' to his own name, Fabian compares him to a hound who can find the fox when the scent is lost: 'The cur is excellent at faults.' For other imagery see page 72.

Because Shakespeare incorporates so much of contemporary Elizabethan life into the play, some examples, readily understood by his audiences, present problems for audiences today. For example, when Sir Andrew says he sent Feste 'sixpence for thy leman', Elizabethans knew at once that the coin was for Feste's sweetheart. They would also know that a 'cheveril glove' was one made of soft leather, and so could be easily turned inside out, an apt image for Feste's view of language itself (Act 3 Scene 1, lines 9–11). Today, such words have to be explained because, like 'cubiculo' (bedroom) and 'yare' (quick), they have fallen out of use.

Similarly, some of the play's references to current affairs or contemporary gossip also require explanation, for example the mention of 'the sophy' (see page 37). Some expressions, like 'Mistress Mall's picture' (Act 1 Scene 3, line 103) and Malvolio's 'the Lady of the Strachy married the yeoman of the wardrobe' (Act 2 Scene 5, lines 34–5), have defeated all attempts at explanation. The most noticeable example of incorporating matters of topical interest occurs in the 66 lines of Act 3 Scene 2:

- Sir Toby's mention of 'grand-jurymen' refers to the practice that only a grand jury could decide if a case had sufficient evidence to proceed to trial.
- Fabian's warning that Sir Andrew has now 'sailed into the north of my lady's opinion' where, unless he performs some act of bravery

he 'will hang like an icicle on a Dutchman's beard' refers to a voyage made to the Arctic in 1596–7 by the Dutchman, William Barents.

- Sir Andrew's protest that he 'had as lief be a Brownist as a politician' refers to the extreme puritan sect founded by Robert Browne in 1581.
- Sir Toby's instruction that Sir Andrew's challenge to Cesario can be written on a piece of paper 'big enough for the bed of Ware in England' refers to the much celebrated Elizabethan bedstead that could sleep eleven persons (which can be seen today in the Victoria and Albert museum in London).
- Maria's description of Malvolio as he practises smiling as the forged letter instructed: 'He does smile his face into more lines than is in the new map with the augmentation of the Indies', refers to a map of India and the Far East published in 1599. It was more detailed than previous maps ('augmentation') and had lines which radiated out from different points like wrinkles around the eyes.

Shakespeare's original audiences would probably have registered and responded to these topical references at a number of levels. For example, most audience members would have known that yellow stockings and cross-garters were already unfashionable around 1600. That knowledge would have added to their enjoyment of Malvolio's humiliation. But it is likely, too, that some would have seen in Malvolio's new costume a satire on a 1597 official proclamation against 'inordinate apparel', ordering subjects to wear the clothes appropriate to their rank (see page 92 for a discussion of similarly subversive interpretations).

In addition to the topical reminders of everyday life described above there are other ways in which *Twelfth Night* reveals what Elizabethan England was like. What follows identifies further social and cultural contexts that influenced the creation of *Twelfth Night*: Twelfth Night festivities, the Elizabethan household, the Fool, madness, love, religion, the theatre.

Twelfth Night festivities

In Elizabethan times, the twelve days after Christmas up to Twelfth Night on 6 January (Epiphany) were traditionally a time of holiday and festival. It was a time for celebration and revelry, sometimes known as the 'Feast of Fools'. Normal behaviour and conventions could be suspended in this period of high jinks. Authority was up-ended. What was usually seen as bad behaviour was tolerated and forgiven. In universities, great country houses and the Inns of Court (the law schools in London), a 'Lord of Misrule' was chosen (often a servant) who became, for a short time, master of the household. He (never she) organised dances, masques and make-believe activities.

The custom of appointing a Lord of Misrule from Christmas Day to Twelfth Night contained elements of Christianity and paganism. Its practice was widespread in Europe for many centuries. Its origins lay in the Saturnalia of ancient Rome, a time when slaves and masters changed places, and a mock king ruled a topsy-turvy world. At the Universities of Oxford and Cambridge, he was known as 'King of the Kingdom of the Bean', a title also used in Holland and Germany. When, in the sixteenth century, the University of Cambridge unsuccessfully tried to suppress the Bean-King and his revelry, 'some grave Governors mentioned the good use thereof, because thereby, in twelve days, they more discover the dispositions of Scholars than in twelve months before'.

All kinds of folly, pranks, and deceptions were allowed in this upside-down world of confusion and masquerades. A never-never land was created, remote from the normal daily world. Illusions, festivities and riotous madness set the mood. Common sense and decorum went out of the window. Pleasure and madness flourished as people were released from their everyday inhibitions. Comedy, disguise, cross-dressing and boisterous frivolity were the order of the day. Traditional authority could be challenged and undermined through carnival (see page 93).

The brief period of festivity allowed people to do as they pleased, and to indulge their fantasies. For a short time, servants could order their masters about. Today, a relic of this custom is the custom in the Army for officers to serve Christmas dinner to the ordinary soldiers. But the major function of the twelve days was to remind the underdogs where power really lay, and that the normal hierarchy would and must be obeyed after the short holiday.

Twelfth Night marked the end of both the Christmas holiday and the holiday season. The next day it was back to the normality of hard work in the everyday world. The short time of pleasure was over. So January 6 was tinged with sadness as the Christmas decorations were taken down and the festivities ended. If Twelfth Night represented a binge, it was also 'the morning after'.

C L Barber's *Shakespeare's Festive Comedy* contains a valuable examination of how the form and practice of Elizabethan holidays, through disguise, merriment, dance and licence, contributed to the dramatic form of festive comedy. The many examples Barber provides (including May games, holiday customs and aristocratic entertainments) provide illuminating contexts for appreciating Sir Toby's behaviour and revelling in *Twelfth Night*. But it is interesting to note that there seems little sense of the festive world in the parts of the play concerned mainly with Orsino, Olivia, Sebastian and Antonio.

The Fool: Feste

Fools were often employed in the palaces of royalty or great houses of noble families. Although they had the title of 'Fool' (or jester or clown), they were much more intelligent than foolish ('a witty fool'). Their job was not simply to provide amusement, but to make critical comment on contemporary behaviour. An 'allowed fool' was able to say what he thought. No punishment would follow: 'there's no slander in an allowed fool'.

Feste is such an 'allowed fool'. He is employed by Olivia, and was a favourite of her father. He gets on well with Sir Toby, and is just as much at home at Duke Orsino's. He is very much his own man, an observer and a sceptic, moving easily between all levels of society in Illyria. Only Malvolio dislikes him, and Feste exacts revenge on the puritanical steward.

The critic Muriel Bradbrook sets Feste in the context of the stage Fools of Elizabethan and Jacobean times. In particular she identifies the actors who played such roles in Shakespeare's own acting company. Throughout the 1590s the company's leading clown was Will Kempe. He played the comic roles of Peter in *Romeo and Juliet* and Dogberry in *Much Ado About Nothing*. When Kempe left the company in 1599, his place was taken by Robert Armin. Bradbrook argues that Armin's distinctive qualities led Shakespeare to create Feste (and such other roles as Touchstone in *As You Like It*, the Gravedigger in *Hamlet*, and the Fool in *King Lear*).

The new feature about these parts is that they are dramatically interwoven with the major characters and the central feelings of a play; they demand an actor to play many parts, not just his own brand of clowning.

Bradbrook notes that Armin's comic roles share the same characteristics: music, song, a deflating wit, and a concern to prove others fools. She argues that Feste is a 'learned fool' in the tradition descending from the 'wise fooling' of Sir Thomas More and Erasmus, rather than the physical humour of more boisterous clowns of popular entertainment. She shows that Armin was proud of his learning, and that Shakespeare incorporated that quality into Feste's inventive talk, his mock authority as Sir Topas, and in his Latin tag to Olivia: '*cucullus non facit monachum*: that's as much to say as I wear not motley in my brain' (Act 1 Scene 5, lines 45–6). Feste may play the Fool, but he is no fool.

Madness

The tormenting of Malvolio in Act 4 Scene 2 reflects Elizabethan beliefs and practices. Shakespeare's contemporaries believed that people showing signs of madness were possessed by devils, and that they should be kept confined in a dark place. It was also a customary 'sport' to visit places where the mentally disturbed were held, and to find pleasure in their antics. Today, such a practice is thought reprehensible, and audiences are troubled by what seems to be the cruel punishment of Malvolio, but it is generally believed that Elizabethans were untroubled by such feelings, and found the tormenting scene amusing.

The Elizabethan household

Orsino and Olivia resemble members of the Elizabethan nobility, wealthy and confident at the head of their extensive estates. Most of the action of the play takes place in or near Olivia's house, which appears strikingly similar to an aristocratic household of Elizabethan England. It contains recognisable characters found in such households. There is the great lady, mistress of her household, her steward and waiting woman, a Fool and assorted hangers-on: a drunken uncle, a foppish wooer. Only the lord of the household is missing: Olivia's dead father or brother.

Malvolio's position, and his behaviour in rebuking Sir Toby's drunken revelling, was rooted in contemporary practice. In 1595 the written instructions to the steward of Viscount Montague ordered him to reprove 'negligent and disordered persons . . . frequenters of tabling, carding and dicing in corners and at untimely hours and seasons'. In Orsino's household, Viola's position as page to Orsino also reflects customary Elizabethan practice: as part of their education, high-status young men often went into a period of service with other noble families.

Love

The very first line announces that love will be a central theme of the play: 'If music be the food of love, play on'. But for many Elizabethans, the notion of love was not that of the modern western ideal in which individuals fall in love and marry simply for personal qualities. Among the Elizabethan aristocracy, and in rich families, marriages were often arranged. Personal choice was far less important than marriages of sons or daughters that would extend or maintain land, wealth and power. This economic reality of arranged marriages was overlaid by two beliefs much written about in stories and plays: courtly love and romantic love.

The literary tradition of courtly love 'put women on a pedestal' and worshipped them from afar as unattainable goddesses. Only by long devotion, many trials and much suffering, could a man win his ideal woman, the 'fair cruel maid' of literature. In Feste's melancholy song to Orsino (Act 2 Scene 4, line 52), the lover dies, rejected by that fair cruel maid. As Feste's song suggests, such a sexless and idealised view of love implies that Orsino is in love with the idea of love itself, rather than with a living woman.

Romantic love was also idealised and unsexual, but it included 'love at first sight', and marriage was its expected outcome. It would seem that Viola falls in love instantly with Orsino (or at least within the three days that Orsino takes Viola-Cesario into his service). Olivia too falls for Cesario at their first meeting: 'Even so quickly may one catch the plague?'

Both kinds of love produced 'the melancholy lover', the man who suffers for his love. He sighs and longs for the woman he adores, but she is always difficult or impossible to attain. Orsino is Shakespeare's presentation of the melancholy lover, in love with the idea of love itself. Changeable and moody ('Enough; no more'), he wallows in his emotions and talks incessantly of love, claiming his own love is greater than anyone else's ('my love, more noble than the world'). He considers himself an authority on love ('such as I am all true lovers are'), and uses the language of exaggeration to describe it ('as hungry as the sea').

Puritanism

'Puritan' was originally used as a term of abuse in the 1560s. But by the time Shakespeare began writing his plays, it had been enthusiastically adopted by those Protestants who considered themselves purer and more perfect and godly than their fellow Christians. Puritans saw themselves as the only true believers. They detested all the show and spectacle and ceremony associated with Catholicism, preferring simplicity in worship and dress. They therefore wanted the reformation of the Church, which had begun under Henry VIII, to go much further, getting rid of bishops, simplifying Church rituals, dress and worship.

The Puritans were extreme in their stinging criticism of swearing, drunkenness and fornication. They condemned maypole dancing, gambling and other popular pursuits. They particularly detested the festivities that went on at Easter, Christmas and Twelfth Night, considering them merely an excuse for people to overeat and get drunk. Sober, self-disciplined and perceived as joyless, the Puritans were also vehemently critical of the stage, denouncing plays and players as immoral and blasphemous. They condemned the cross-dressing boys who played women's roles, claiming the practice provoked illicit sexual desires in audiences.

In the light of such puritanical attitudes, it is easy to understand why *Twelfth Night* is sometimes interpreted as Shakespeare's criticism of puritanism, represented in the character of Malvolio. Such a claim is impossible to prove or disprove, but it is clear that the play portrays contending values in Elizabethan England: puritan austerity versus hedonistic enjoyment ('cakes and ale').

Shakespeare's own life

This section began with the film *Shakespeare in Love*. It is a delightful fantasy which gives the impression that the inspiration for *Romeo and Juliet* was Shakespeare's own personal experience of falling in love (and its ending strongly suggests *Twelfth Night*'s Viola on Illyria's seashore). Today, critics and examiners give little or no credit to approaches which interpret *Twelfth Night* in the context of

Shakespeare's emotional life, because nothing is really known of his intimate thoughts, feelings or activities.

Nonetheless, some critics who discuss *Twelfth Night* have made much of the fact that Shakespeare himself had twin children. They claim that the death in 1596 of one twin, the eleven-year-old Hamnet, was much on his mind as he wrote the play, accounting for *Twelfth Night*'s melancholy tone (and for the tragedies which followed). Such a claim is neither provable nor disprovable, and today the focus of critical attention is on social and cultural contexts such as those identified in this section.

An important critical question about those contexts concerns Shakespeare's attitude to them: what was his personal view of the practices, conventions and values of the time? What was his attitude to love, to puritanism or to the aristocracy (or even to such matters as bear-baiting)? Is the play a subtle and ironic critique of male power, showing that even such a spirited, independent and capable female as Viola finally accepts the dominance of a male who has shown little but self-centred indulgence for most of the play? Once again, no one really knows for certain. But as this section shows, what is clear is that *Twelfth Night* is richly influenced by many features of Elizabethan England. And as the section on Critical approaches will show (pages 81–103), it is possible to construct persuasive arguments to support very different interpretations of the attitude of the play (or Shakespeare's) to the various contextual features and issues that the play dramatises.

Language

Ben Jonson famously remarked that Shakespeare 'wanted art' (lacked technical skill). But Jonson's comment is mistaken, as is the popular image of Shakespeare as a 'natural' writer, utterly spontaneous, inspired only by his imagination. Shakespeare possessed a profound knowledge of the language techniques of his own and previous times. Behind the apparent effortlessness of the language lies a deeply practised skill. That skill is evident in *Twelfth Night* in all kinds of ways. The play displays a wide variety of language registers, and the songs subtly echo the play's themes and moods. The pervasive wordplay reflects the confusions and dramatic irony that arise from mistaken appearance; it constantly reminds the audience of the duplicity of language.

What follows are some of the language techniques Shakespeare uses in *Twelfth Night* to intensify dramatic effect, create mood and character, and so produce memorable theatre. As you read them, always keep in mind that Shakespeare wrote for the stage, and that actors will therefore employ a wide variety of both verbal and non-verbal methods to exploit the dramatic possibilities of the language. They will use the full range of their voices and accompany the words with appropriate expressions, gestures and actions.

Imagery

Twelfth Night abounds in imagery (sometimes called 'figures' or 'figurative language'): vivid words and phrases that help create the atmosphere of the play as they conjure up emotionally-charged mental pictures in the imagination. When Antonio says that his desire 'More sharp than filèd steel, did spur me forth' to follow Sebastian, the sharp, piercing and painful nature of Antonio's feelings for his friend is acutely conveyed in the imagery. As both a poet and a playwright, Shakespeare seems to have thought in images, and the whole play richly demonstrates his unflagging and varied use of verbal illustration right from its opening line 'If music be the food of love, play on'.

Early critics, such as John Dryden and Doctor Johnson, were critical of Shakespeare's fondness for imagery. They felt that many images obscured meaning and detracted attention from the subjects they represented. Over the past 200 years, however, critics, poets and audiences have increasingly valued Shakespeare's imagery. They recognise how he uses it to give pleasure as it stirs the audience's imagination, deepens the dramatic impact of particular moments or moods, provides insight into character, and intensifies meaning and emotional force. Images carry powerful significance far deeper than their surface meanings.

As the section on Contexts shows, Shakespeare's Elizabethan world provides much of the play's imagery. For example, pages 62–3 note many images of hunting and entrapment. Another such image, familiar to Elizabethans, occurs when Malvolio thinks he has truly captured Olivia's affections: 'I have limed her' (Act 3 Scene 4, line 66). The image is from the cruel contemporary practice of trapping birds with sticky lime spread on tree branches. Elsewhere, animals and birds provide a rich source of images. Sir Toby praises Maria as 'a beagle, true bred', Fabian says Viola 'looks pale, as if a bear were at his heels', Orsino angrily describes Viola as a 'dissembling cub', having threatened to treat her as a sacrificial lamb, and imagines Olivia as a dove with the heart of a raven:

> I'll sacrifice the lamb that I do love,
> To spite a raven's heart within a dove.
>
> *(Act 5 Scene 1, lines 119–20)*

Shakespeare's imagery uses metaphor, simile or personification. All are comparisons which, in effect, substitute one thing (the image) for another (the thing described).

- A *simile* compares one thing to another using 'like' or 'as'. Sir Toby says that Sir Andrew's hair 'hangs like flax on a distaff', and Orsino recalls Antonio's face in the sea-battle: 'it was besmeared /As black as Vulcan' (the Roman god of fire, blacksmith to the gods).
- A *metaphor* is also a comparison, suggesting that two dissimilar things are actually the same. When Sir Toby demands of Malvolio 'Dost thou think because thou art virtuous there shall be no more cakes and ale?', the seemingly simple image of 'cakes and ale' is a striking metaphor for a whole world of celebration, festivity and hedonistic enjoyment.

To put it another way, a metaphor borrows one word or phrase to express another. For example, Feste describes Orsino's mind as 'a very opal'. The image of an iridescent precious stone that changes colour with the light precisely catches the Duke's changeability and inconstant nature that Orsino had himself described a few lines earlier.

• *Personification* turns all kinds of things into persons, giving them human feelings or attributes. Viola memorably personifies Patience in one of the play's most famous descriptions which is rich in all three kinds of imagery:

> She never told her love,
> But let concealment like a worm i'th'bud
> Feed on her damask cheek. She pined in thought,
> And with a green and yellow melancholy
> She sat like Patience on a monument,
> Smiling at grief.   *(Act 2 Scene 4, lines 106–11)*

Classical mythology contributes to the richness of the play's imagery. Elizabethans were usually more familiar with such references than most members of audiences are today. In the first scene they would recognise that Orsino's image of being turned into a deer pursued by savage hounds arises from a story in Ovid's *Metamorphoses*. The hunter Actaeon saw the goddess Diana bathing. As punishment, he was turned into a stag and chased and killed by his own hunting dogs.

Similarly, Elizabethans, knowing that Jove is a god famous for his exploits in love, would find it appropriate that Malvolio thanks Jove for helping him (as he mistakenly believes) win the love of Olivia. In the same way, they would appreciate the humorous inappropriateness of Sir Toby's calling the diminutive Maria Penthesilea (Queen of the Amazons). When, in Act 3 Scene 1, Feste begs another tip from Viola by saying 'I would play Lord Pandarus of Phrygia, sir, to bring a Cressida to this Troilus', many of Shakespeare's contemporaries would share Viola's response: 'I understand you sir'. For them, the classical story of Pandarus who brought the Trojan and Greek lovers together was well known, most probably through Chaucer's love poem *Troilus and Criseyde*. (It should perhaps be noted that the love of Troilus and Cressida, together with the creation of Pandarus as pander, are medieval additions to the story of Troy.)

Antithesis

Antithesis is the opposition of words or phrases against each other, as when Viola exclaims about Olivia 'But if you were the devil, you are fair!' or when Fabian, looking for forgiveness for the trick he and the others have played on Malvolio, hopes it 'May rather pluck on laughter than revenge'. This setting of word against word ('devil' stands in contrast to 'fair', 'laughter' opposes 'revenge') is one of Shakespeare's favourite language devices. He uses it extensively in all his plays. Why? Because antithesis powerfully expresses conflict through its use of opposites, and conflict is the essence of all drama.

In *Twelfth Night*, conflict occurs in many forms: the formality of Orsino's elegant court versus the more relaxed household of Olivia; Malvolio's uptight puritanism versus Sir Toby's carefree revels; Olivia's resistance to Orsino's wooing; Viola's 'barful strife' – her emotional struggle as her love for Orsino clashes with her duty to act as his love-messenger to Olivia. Even more strikingly perhaps, throughout the play there are many conflicts of reality and appearance: a girl mistaken for a boy, one twin for another, a forged letter for a true declaration of love. Nothing is quite what it seems in this play of mistaken identity. Viola's remark to the Captain 'that nature with a beauteous wall / Doth oft close in pollution', and her declaration to Olivia that 'I am not what I am', are just two antitheses that express the conflict between outward show and inward reality.

Antithesis intensifies the sense of conflict, and embodies its different forms. In the 'duel' scene (Act 3 Scene 4) Viola, preferring peace to duelling, says she would 'rather go with sir priest than sir knight', and Antonio, mistaking Viola for Cesario and feeling betrayed, vehemently exclaims 'O how vile an idol proves this god!' Absurdly wooing Olivia, Malvolio dismisses Maria as unworthy of an answer: 'nightingales answer daws!' With a similar sense of opposing qualities, Olivia dismisses Orsino's protestations of love as distasteful to her 'as howling after music'. Feste, pretending to be Sir Topas, uses three antitheses to describe the dark room in which the hapless Malvolio is imprisoned:

> Why, it hath bay windows transparent as barricadoes, and the clerestories toward the south-north are as lustrous as ebony
>
> *(Act 4 Scene 2, lines 30–1)*

Feste's deliberately confusing antitheses are reminders that the genre of *Twelfth Night* is comedy. Shakespeare therefore ensures that conflicts result in humour rather than, as in the histories and tragedies, in unhappiness and death. Conflict is comic, and the many uses of antithesis contribute to audience enjoyment. Much of that pleasure comes from relishing the dramatic irony that arises from the antitheses describing different kinds of mistaken identity, as when Olivia says to the ludicrously transformed Malvolio 'Smil'st thou? I sent for thee upon a sad occasion', or when Sebastian declares Olivia 'betrothed both to a maid and man'.

Repetition

Different forms of language repetition run through the play, contributing to its atmosphere, creation of character and dramatic impact. Apart from familiar grammatical words ('the', 'and', etc.) the two lexical words most frequently repeated are 'love' (used nearly 80 times), and 'mad', 'madman' or 'madness' (40 times). Their repetition is a clear indication of the major preoccupations of the play.

Repetition is a distinctive feature of Sir Andrew Aguecheek's style. To emphasise Andrew's dimwittedness, Shakespeare often has Andrew repeat another character's words or sentiments, as for example on his first appearance ('I would I might never draw sword again') or when he can do little more than echo Sir Toby's congratulations to Maria after her forged letter has successfully deceived Malvolio (Act 2 Scene 5, lines 155–71).

Shakespeare's skill in using repetition to heighten theatrical effect and deepen emotional and imaginative significance is most evident in particular speeches. Repeated words, phrases, rhythms and sounds add intensity to the moment or episode. For example, the letter's mantra 'Some are born great, some achieve greatness, and some have greatness thrust upon 'em' is repeated with knowing delight by Malvolio to Olivia as he woos her. It is repeated again towards the end of the play, this time mockingly by Feste to increase Malvolio's humiliation. Elsewhere, a single repeated word contributes power to Viola's protestation that she loves Orsino:

> More than I love these eyes, more than my life,
> More, by all mores, than e'er I shall love wife.
> *(Act 5 Scene 1, lines 124–5)*

The repeated rhythms of verse are discussed later (see page 79), but the play's prose also contains the same qualities of rhythmical and phrase repetition, as for example in Feste's various parodies of logic (Act 1 Scene 5, lines 45–59; Act 2 Scene 3, lines 23–5; Act 4 Scene 2, lines 11–14), Malvolio's delight in his belief that Olivia loves him (Act 2 Scene 5, lines 133–47), and Sir Toby's rhythmical questions in Act 1 Scene 3: 'Wherefore are these things hid? Wherefore have these gifts a curtain before 'em?' (lines 102–8). The same subtle rhythmical and lexical repetitions are found in the prose dialogue between Viola and Olivia on their first meeting (Act 1 Scene 5, lines 139–94).

Repetition also occasionally occurs in rhyme, nearly always in couplets to close a scene or episode. There is space to give only a few examples to suggest how these rhyming couplets achieve a variety of effects and moods, for example in conveying Orsino's self-indulgence:

> Away before me to sweet beds of flowers:
> Love-thoughts lie rich when canopied with bowers.
>
> *(Act 1 Scene 1, lines 40–1)*

or Antonio's passionate feelings for Sebastian:

> But come what may, I do adore thee so
> That danger shall seem sport, and I will go.
>
> *(Act 2 Scene 1, lines 35–6)*

or the disguised Viola's puzzled acceptance of the strange situation she finds herself in because of Olivia's love:

> O time, thou must untangle this, not I;
> It is too hard a knot for me t'untie.   *(Act 2 Scene 2, lines 37–8)*

or Sebastian's wonder at the fantastic events that have just happened to him:

> What relish is in this? How runs the stream?
> Or I am mad, or else this is a dream.
> Let fancy still my sense in Lethe steep;
> If it be thus to dream, still let me sleep!
>
> *(Act 4 Scene 1, lines 53–6)*

It is a valuable activity to check through the play, identifying how Shakespeare achieves different effects through rhyming couplets at the end of scenes or episodes. But it should also be noted that Shakespeare self-consciously parodies the practice when he has Sir Toby mockingly say (in prose), having heard Viola use such couplets:

> Come hither, knight, come hither, Fabian. We'll whisper o'er
> a couplet or two of most sage saws.'
>
> *(Act 3 Scene 4, lines 328–9)*

Lists

One of Shakespeare's favourite language methods is to accumulate words or phrases rather like a list. He had learned the technique as a schoolboy in Stratford-upon-Avon, and his skill in knowing how to use lists dramatically is evident in the many examples in *Twelfth Night*. He intensifies and varies description, atmosphere and argument as he 'piles up' item on item, incident on incident. Sometimes the list comprises only single words or phrases, as in Sir Toby's contemptuous rejection of Sir Andrew:

> an ass-head, and a coxcomb, and a knave, a thin-faced knave, a
> gull   *(Act 5 Scene 1, lines 190–1)*

or Viola's condemnation of ingratitude:

> I hate ingratitude more in a man
> Than lying, vainness, babbling drunkenness,
> Or any taint of vice   *(Act 3 Scene 4, lines 305–7)*

Some lists are brief descriptions ('the most skilful, bloody, and fatal opposite', 'fashion, colour, ornament'). Others are more extended character portrayals, as in Olivia's praise of Orsino:

> Yet I suppose him virtuous, know him noble,
> Of great estate, of fresh and stainless youth;
> In voices well divulged, free, learned, and valiant
>
> *(Act 1 Scene 5, lines 213–15)*

or in Sebastian's recognition of Olivia's qualities:

> She could not sway her house, command her followers,
> Take and give back affairs and them dispatch,
> With such a smooth, discreet, and stable bearing
> As I perceive she does. *(Act 4 Scene 3, lines 17–20)*

One special type of list appearing in different forms in *Twelfth Night* is the blazon, a technique of romantic poetry that itemised and idealised the features of a loved one. Olivia names it as such as she thinks about Cesario:

> Thy tongue, thy face, thy limbs, actions, and spirit
> Do give thee five-fold blazon. *(Act 1 Scene 5, lines 247–8)*

But elsewhere, Shakespeare seems to parody the technique of the blazon (and of lists in general), as when Olivia mockingly catalogues her features:

> It shall be inventoried and every particle and utensil labelled to my will, as, *item*, two lips, indifferent red; *item*, two grey eyes, with lids to them; *item*, one neck, one chin, and so forth.
> *(Act 1 Scene 5, lines 201–4)*

and when Maria, planning the forged letter that will deceive Malvolio, describes how he will identify himself in it:

> by the colour of his beard, the shape of his leg, the manner of his gait, the expressure of his eye, forehead, and complexion
> *(Act 2 Scene 3, lines 132–3)*

The many lists in the play provide valuable opportunities for actors to vary their delivery. In speaking, a character usually seeks to give each 'item' a distinctiveness in emphasis and emotional tone, and sometimes an accompanying action and expression. In addition, the accumulating effect of lists can add to the force of argument, enrich atmosphere, amplify meaning and provide extra dimensions of character.

Verse and prose

About one-third of the play is in verse, two-thirds are in prose. How did Shakespeare decide whether to write in verse or prose? One answer is that he followed theatrical convention. Prose was traditionally used by comic and low-status characters. High-status characters spoke verse. 'Comic' scenes were written in prose (as were letters, like the one Maria forges to trick Malvolio), but audiences expected verse in 'serious' scenes: the poetic style was thought to be particularly suitable for lovers and for moments of high dramatic or emotional intensity.

Shakespeare used his judgement about which convention or principle he should follow in *Twelfth Night*, and it is obvious that he frequently broke the 'rules'. Viola (high-status) switches frequently from verse to prose, and her first dialogue with Olivia (also high-status) is in prose. Sir Toby and Sir Andrew always use prose. They too are high-status characters, but their dramatic function is comic. Further, the style of prose in the play displays great variation, for example in Malvolio's soliloquies in Act 2 Scene 5, Feste's clever word-play, and Sir Toby's language, sometimes witty, sometimes slurred with drink.

The verse of *Twelfth Night* is similarly varied, but it is mainly in blank verse: unrhymed verse written in iambic pentameter. It is conventional to define iambic pentameter as a rhythm or metre in which each line has five stressed syllables (/) alternating with five unstressed syllables (×):

> × / × / × / × / × /
> Disguise, I see thou art a wickedness

At school, Shakespeare had learned the technical definition of iambic pentameter. In Greek, *penta* means five, and *iamb* means a 'foot' of two syllables, the first unstressed, the second stressed, as in 'alas' = aLAS. Shakespeare practised writing in that metre, and his early plays, such as *Titus Andronicus* and *Richard III* are very regular in rhythm (often expressed as de-DUM de-DUM de-DUM de-DUM de-DUM), and with each line 'end-stopped' (making sense on its own).

By the time he came to write *Twelfth Night* (around 1600), Shakespeare had become very flexible and experimental in his use of iambic pentameter. The 'five-beat' rhythm is still present, but less prominent. End-stopped lines are less frequent. There is greater use of *enjambement* (running on), where one line flows on into the next, seemingly with little or no pause, as in Orsino's lines:

> How will she love, when the rich golden shaft
> Hath killed the flock of all affections else
> That live in her   *(Act 1 Scene 1, lines 35–7)*

Some critics, directors and actors have strong convictions about how the verse should be spoken. For example, the director Peter Hall insists there should always be a pause at the end of each line. But it seems appropriate when studying (or watching or acting in) *Twelfth Night*, not to attempt to apply rigid rules about verse-speaking. Shakespeare certainly used the convention of iambic pentameter, but he did not adhere to it slavishly. He knew 'the rules', but he was not afraid to break them to suit his dramatic purposes. No one knows for sure just how the lines were delivered on Shakespeare's own stage, and today actors use their discretion in how to deliver the lines. They pause or emphasise to convey meaning and emotion and to avoid the mechanical or clockwork-sounding speech that a too slavish attention to the pentameter line might produce.

Traditional criticism

Twelfth Night seems to have been a popular play right from the time it was first performed. John Manningham's enjoyment of a performance in 1602 has been noted on page 57. His particular enjoyment of the Malvolio plot seems to have been shared by others. In 1632 King Charles I wrote 'Malvolio' in place of the play's title in his own copy of the play, and in 1640 Leonard Digges praised Shakespeare in verses which included the following lines testifying to Malvolio's box-office appeal:

> lo in a trice
> The Cockpit Galleries, Boxes, all are full
> To hear Malvolio that cross-gartered Gull.

But the diarist Samuel Pepys was not impressed by the play. His diary entry for 6 January 1663 reads:

> To the Duke's house, and there saw Twelfth-Night acted well, though it be but a silly play, and not relating at all to the name or day.

The comments of Manningham, Digges and Pepys are little more than passing mentions. In contrast, sustained critical writing on the play is usually agreed to begin with the leading eighteenth-century critic Doctor Samuel Johnson. He embodies the tradition of his time, which attempted to find moral instruction in the theatre. Johnson praised *Twelfth Night*, and was especially taken with Malvolio's soliloquy, seeing it as an example of pride leading to ridicule, and so 'truly comic'. Elsewhere, however, Johnson's censorious tone expresses concern about the play's lack of truthfulness to real life and failure to provide moral lessons:

> This play is in the graver part elegant and easy, and in some of the lighter scenes exquisitely humorous . . . The marriage of Olivia, and the succeeding perplexity, though well enough

contrived to divert on the stage, wants credibility, and fails to produce the proper instruction required in the drama, as it exhibits no just picture of life.

Johnson's concern to find moral teaching in theatre is clearly concerned with characters, judging them as if they were real persons. From the late eighteenth century, through the nineteenth, and well into the twentieth, that focus on moral judgement and character has continued in critical writing about *Twelfth Night*. Two well-known passages by William Hazlitt illustrate the tradition. Both are from his significantly titled *The Characters of Shakespeare's Plays*, 1817. First, a judgement on how *Twelfth Night* develops moral insights:

> This is justly considered as one of the most delightful of Shakespeare's comedies. It is full of sweetness and pleasantry. It is perhaps too good-natured for comedy. It has little satire, and no spleen. It aims at the ludicrous rather than the ridiculous. It makes us laugh at the follies of mankind, not despise them, and still less bear any ill-will towards them.

Second, a discussion which claims to show how those moral insights emerge from audiences' attitudes to characters:

> The great and secret charm of *Twelfth Night* is the character of Viola. Much as we like catches and cakes and ale, there is something we like better. We have a friendship for Sir Toby; we patronise Sir Andrew; we have an understanding with the Clown, a sneaking kindness for Maria and her rogueries; we feel a regard for Malvolio, and sympathise with his gravity, his smiles, his cross garters, his yellow stockings, and imprisonment in the stocks. But there is something that excites in us a stronger feeling than all this – it is Viola's confession of her love.

Hazlitt's style is typical of a great deal of traditional character criticism. One aspect calls for immediate comment: his use of the first person plural ('we', 'us', 'our'). It is a style that has bedevilled critical writing right up to the present time. Like all critics who use 'we', Hazlitt was reporting his own personal response to the play, but attempting to pass it off as something everybody feels (or should feel). Such use of language is suspect, because many people simply do not share the sympathies expressed. Not everyone feels 'friendship' for Sir Toby, or that they 'patronise' Sir Andrew and so on. As noted later in this Guide (see pages 113 and 115), the use of 'we', 'our', etc. is best avoided in your own writing.

Hazlitt's character criticism places Viola at the centre of attention. That focus was quickly challenged by his contemporary, Charles Lamb. He, like the earliest commentators on the play mentioned above, saw Malvolio as the centre of dramatic interest. But, unlike their enjoyment of the humour in Malvolio's discomfiture, Lamb felt that Malvolio had been much misunderstood, and he detected other qualities in Olivia's steward:

> Malvolio is not essentially ludicrous. he becomes comic but by accident. He is cold, austere, repelling; but dignified . . . his pride or his gravity (call it which you will) is inherent, and native to the man, not mock or affected, which latter only are the fit objects to excite laughter. His quality is at the best unlovely, but neither buffoon nor contemptible . . . we see no reason why he should not have been brave, honourable, accomplished.

Lamb argued that Malvolio rightly felt that the honour of Olivia's household was in his keeping, and that there was 'no room for laughter' in his gulling. Lamb's emphasis on the integrity of the character influenced later performances of the role. Perhaps the most notable example was the portrayal in 1884 by Sir Henry Irving, whose gaunt and sober Malvolio possessed an innate dignity which added pathos to his humiliation.

Hazlitt and Lamb and other Romantic critics effectively set the tone for nineteenth-century criticism of *Twelfth Night* in its preoccupation with character. But the critic with whom the expression 'character study' is most associated is A C Bradley. Around 100 years ago, Bradley delivered a course of lectures at Oxford University which were published in 1904 as *Shakespearean Tragedy*. The book has never been out of print, and Bradley's approach has been hugely influential.

Although Bradley makes only passing references to *Twelfth Night* (he is centrally concerned with *Hamlet, Macbeth, Othello* and *King*

Lear), his form of criticism reflects previous approaches to the play, and has strongly influenced critical approaches right up to the present day. Bradley talks about the characters in Shakespeare's plays as if they were real human beings, experiencing familiar human emotions and thoughts, and existing in worlds recognisable to modern readers. He identifies the unique desires and motives which give characters their particular personalities, and which evoke feelings of admiration or disapproval in the audience.

Bradley's character approach has been much criticised, particularly for its neglect of the Elizabethan contexts of the play's creation: the cultural and intellectual assumptions of the time, stage conditions, and poetic and dramatic conventions. But Bradley's distinctive contribution to *Twelfth Night* character criticism was to shift its focus from Malvolio and Viola to Feste, whom he saw as a distinctively modern figure, wholeheartedly devoted to his profession, unable to make personal relationships, dependent on 'insensitive patrons', but with a sane and realistic attitude to the absurdities of Illyria.

Bradley argues that Feste's name signifies *Twelfth Night*'s concern with festivity, and that his songs and witticisms express the themes of the play. Bradley calls him 'our wise, happy, melodious fool' who links the love plot and the comic plot of the play, appearing in both. It should be noted that Bradley also typically uses the highly misleading first person plural claiming that his opinions are shared by everyone. For example that Feste 'begs so amusingly that we welcome his begging', and that:

> We never laugh at Feste . . . He is as sane as his mistress . . .
> being lord of himself, he cares little for Fortune. His mistress
> may turn him away; but, 'to be turned away, let summer bear
> it out'. This 'sunshine of the breast' is always with him and
> spreads its radiance over the whole scene in which he moves.
> And so we love him.

Bradley's 'And so we love him' is typical of an earlier criticism that assumed immediate agreement by its readers. As will become clear later, modern responses to Feste are more complex, far less sentimental, and much more open to a contradictory range of responses. However, the most frequent objection to Bradley is his treatment of characters as real people. Modern criticism is uneasy about discussing characters in this way, preferring to see them as fictional creations in a stage drama.

Although Bradley has fallen from critical favour, his influence is still evident. As pages 119–24 show, it is difficult to avoid talking or writing about characters as if they were living people and making moral judgements on them. But even in traditional criticism different approaches exist, for example when a character is interpreted as embodying the themes of the play or highlighting thematic aspects of other characters. Thus Harold Jenkins comments:

> The love-delusions of Malvolio, brilliant as they are, fall into perspective as a parody of the more delicate aberrations of his mistress and her suitor. Like them, Malvolio aspires towards an illusory ideal of love, but his mistake is a grosser one than theirs, his posturings more extravagant and grotesque. So his illusion enlarges the suggestions of the main plot about the mind's capacity for self-deception.

Caroline Spurgeon opened up a further critical perspective on *Twelfth Night*: the study of its imagery. In her book *Shakespeare's Imagery and What it Tells Us*, Spurgeon identifies patterns of imagery in each of Shakespeare's plays. She finds that in *Twelfth Night*:

> The types of images reflect subtly and accurately the rather peculiar mixture of tones in the play, music, romance, sadness and beauty interwoven with wit, broad comedy and quick-moving snappy dialogue.

Spurgeon notes, in prose scenes with Sir Toby, particular images drawn from Elizabethan England ('parish top', 'bum bailey', 'sheriff's post', 'the new map of the Indies', 'the bed of Ware', etc.). She comments that their lightness and brilliance delighted early audiences, and kept alive 'the atmosphere of repartee and topical fun which is one of the characteristics of this sophisticated and delicious comedy'. Elsewhere she remarks on the 'inimitable pictures' in other images such as 'you are sailed into the north of my lady's affection where you will hang like an icicle on a Dutchman's beard'.

It should be noted here that although the value of Caroline Spurgeon's pioneering study of Shakespeare's imagery has been acknowledged by later critics, her work has also been much criticised. For example, she seriously underestimates the sheer amount of imagery in *Twelfth Night*, only occasionally examines how the imagery relates to the dramatic context of the play, and almost invariably uses a tone of praise, avoiding any critical appraisal of the play's imagery. In this she echoes the 'bardolatry' that has dogged Shakespeare criticism ever since the Romantics of the early nineteenth century. Notwithstanding such flaws, her work is immensely valuable in encouraging the study of imagery which is such a distinctive feature of every Shakespeare play. You can find more on imagery in the section on Language (pages 71–3).

A quite different critical approach is that of Muriel Bradbrook, who showed how Feste related to other stage Fools of Elizabethan and Jacobean times, and how his particular style of humour was conditioned by the actor Robert Armin, who first played the role. Bradbrook's arguments are discussed on page 66 of this Guide. Here it must be noted that her judgement of *Twelfth Night* as 'complete and beautifully balanced in itself between the world of revels and the January cold', hints at yet another traditional critical approach to the play: one which detects unity of dramatic design.

Examples of that dramatic unity include Neville Coghill's view of Shakespeare's 'comic vision' as 'the firm assertion of basic harmony', and G Wilson Knight's identification of the imaginative and emotional unity in the love plot of *Twelfth Night*. Wilson Knight identifies a thematic pattern of 'music, love, and precious stones, threaded by the sombre strands of a sea-tempest and a sea-flight', which eventually leads to 'love, reunion and joy'. Other well-known studies which discover artistic unity in *Twelfth Night* are those of H B Charlton in *Shakespearean Comedy* and C L Barber in *Shakespeare's Festive Comedy*.

Charlton argues that *Twelfth Night* possesses a dramatic unity in which its poise and balance reflects and embodies a coherent set of values. Charlton approaches the comedies through their heroines. He employs traditional character criticism (Viola is modest, possesses intuitive insight and judgement, is a quick learner, and so on), but argues that Viola displays an equilibrium of feeling, wit and intelligence which is reflected in the total dramatic design of the play itself. For Charlton, the different parts of *Twelfth Night* are integrated with equipoise and grace into a harmoniously balanced whole:

The rich variety of theme, of episode, and of person . . . is knit together and holds as a coherent structure.

Charlton claims that such coherence (in Viola and in the whole play) shows that *Twelfth Night* is largely occupied with 'the disclosure of unbalanced sentiment' in 'less stable creatures'. For example Orsino possesses 'enervating sentimentality', Olivia displays 'unrestrained emotionalism', Malvolio has 'lost the art of life' and 'the springs of sympathy are dried up within him'. In a style that recalls Doctor Johnson's hope for moral lessons in drama, Charlton concludes:

> Comedy is seeking in its own artistic way to elucidate the moral art of securing happiness by translating the stubbornness of fortune into a quiet and a sweet existence. It finds that this art comes most easily to those who by nature are generous, guiltless, and of a free disposition, just indeed, as are Shakespeare's heroines. It finds the art crippled if not destroyed, in those who lack the genial sense of fellowship with mankind. A Malvolio sick of self-love.

C L Barber is similarly concerned with finding artistic unity and patterns in *Twelfth Night*. Using a concept ('through release to clarification') which he asserts characterises the dramatic movement of other festive comedies, Barber argues that

> Shakespeare's whole handling of romantic story, farce, and practical joke makes a composition which moves in the manner of his earlier festive comedies, through release to clarification.

Barber therefore sees *Twelfth Night* as dealing with 'the folly of misrule', but with characters moving from kinds of 'madness' to sanity. The play shows characters caught up in delusions or misapprehensions which 'bring out what they would keep hidden or did not know was there' and are resolved by 'the finding of objects appropriate to passions': for example when Orsino finally loves Viola.

Barber argues that in the play's 'exhibition of the use and abuse of social liberty', Shakespeare uses Renaissance ideals of courtesy and decorum. Drawing on Renaissance humanist interest in the fashioning of courtiers through appropriate behaviours (decorum), Barber identifies the considerable talk in the play of courtesy and manners, and asserts that Viola successfully achieves her disguise through 'perfect courtesy'.

In contrast, Malvolio, lacking the 'free disposition' that is the basis of courtesy and festive liberty, comes off badly. In the play's design, Malvolio acts as a foil to other characters. His desire to lord it over others threatens to violate decorum. But the festive spirit (for example in Sir Toby's 'Dost thou think because thou art virtuous there shall be no more cakes and ale?') exposes the killjoy vanity of Malvolio's own decorum. Barber's conclusion displays the moralising tendency of much traditional criticism. He sees *Twelfth Night* and other festive comedies having the power to move audiences

> through release to clarification, making distinctions between false care and true freedom and realizing anew, for successive generations, powers in human nature and society which makes good the risks of courtesy and liberty.

Even though Barber, Charlton and other critics take different approaches to *Twelfth Night*, they generally share Bradley's assumptions about character criticism. Harold Bloom is the most recent critic to write in that tradition. In *Shakespeare: The Invention of the Human*, Bloom argues that Shakespeare's characters provided the self-reflexive models by which human beings first acquired selves to reflect on (or to put it more simply, Shakespeare's characters first showed us how to think about ourselves). That enormous claim about the origin of our subjectivity is disputed by almost all scholars, many of whom are dismissive of Bloom's character-study approach as gushing and exaggerated.

Bloom's overriding concern with character is evident. He regards Orsino as 'egregious', remarks on Olivia's 'erotic arbitrariness', sees Maria as a 'high-spirited social climber', and Sir Toby as a 'fifth-rate rascal'. He claims that Feste is 'benign' throughout the play, and judges Viola 'disconcerting'. He asserts that Shakespeare seems to enjoy keeping Viola 'an enigma, with much always held in reserve'. For Bloom, *Twelfth Night* has become Malvolio's play, but because the steward is more victim of his own psychic propensities than he is Maria's gull. Bloom thinks the gulling of Malvolio 'passes into the domain of sadism', and, using the seductive consensual style of so much traditional criticism, he asserts

> Our sympathy is bound to be limited, particularly because of the high hilarity his discomfiture provokes in us.

Modern criticism

Throughout the second half of the twentieth century and in the twenty-first, critical approaches to Shakespeare have radically challenged the style and assumptions of the traditional approaches described above. New critical approaches argue that traditional interpretations, with their focus on character, are individualistic and misleading. The traditional concentration on personal feelings ignores society and history, and so divorces literary, dramatic and aesthetic matters from their social context. Further, their detachment from the real world makes them elitist, sexist and unpolitical.

Modern critical perspectives therefore shift the focus from individuals to how social conditions (of the world of the play and of Shakespeare's England) are reflected in characters' relationships, language and behaviour. Modern criticism also concerns itself with how changing social assumptions at different periods of time have affected interpretations of the play.

It is significant, however, to note that *Twelfth Night*, like other comedies (apart from *The Merchant of Venice*), has attracted less radical critical attention than the tragedies. Further, certain aspects of modern criticism have featured strongly in traditional criticism of *Twelfth Night* (notably in identifying the Elizabethan contexts and relevance of the play, and in some questioning of its unity and 'happy ending'). This section will explore how recent critical approaches to Shakespeare have been and can be used to address *Twelfth Night*. Like traditional criticism, contemporary perspectives include many different approaches but share common features. Modern criticism:

- is sceptical of 'character' approaches (but often uses them – see pages 119–24);
- concentrates on political, social and economic factors (arguing that these factors determine Shakespeare's creativity and audiences' and critics' interpretations);

- identifies contradictions, fragmentation and disunity in the plays;
- questions the possibility of 'happy' or 'hopeful' endings, preferring ambiguous, unsettling or sombre endings;
- produces readings that are subversive of existing social structures;
- identifies how the plays express the interests of dominant groups, particularly rich and powerful males;
- insists that 'theory' (psychological, social, etc.) is essential to produce valid readings;
- often expresses its commitment to a particular cause or perspective (for example, to feminism, or equality, or political change);
- argues all readings are political or ideological readings (and that traditional criticism falsely claims to be objective);
- argues that traditional approaches have always interpreted Shakespeare conservatively, in ways that confirm and maintain the interests of the elite or dominant class.

The following discussion is organised under headings which represent major contemporary critical perspectives (political, feminist, performance, psychoanalytic, postmodern). But it is vital to appreciate that there is often overlap between the categories, and that to pigeonhole any example of criticism too precisely is to reduce its value and application.

Political criticism

'Political criticism' is a convenient label for approaches concerned with power and social structure in the world of the play, in Shakespeare's time and in our own. At first sight, *Twelfth Night* appears to be resistant to such interpretations, being centrally concerned with such matters as love, disguise and mistaken identity. Nonetheless, various interpretations, both in criticism and in stage productions, have highlighted 'political' aspects of the play. For example, the Marxist critic Elliot Krieger (partly reacting to Barber's arguments, see page 87) highlights the importance of social class, and argues that 'a ruling-class ideology operates within the play'. He asserts that the expression 'all is fortune' is part of that ruling-class ideology, used and intended to keep the working class blind to the fact that it is people, not fortune, who bring about changes in society. Krieger claims that *Twelfth Night* does not dramatise strategies of bourgeois opposition so much as of aristocratic protection. Only a privileged social class has access to the morality of indulgence: if the members of the ruling class find their identities through excessive indulgence in appetite, the other characters in the play either work to make indulgence possible for their superiors, or else, indulging themselves, sicken and so die.

Other 'political' critics have focused on often unremarked aspects of Illyria: trade wars which result in bloody combat, officers watching for political enemies of the state, Orsino's role as military leader. In consequence, some modern productions have portrayed Illyria as a feudal, male-dominated society, exercising control through licensed foolery. Elsewhere, critics have argued that both Malvolio and Sir Andrew are strongly motivated by considerations of wealth and power in their wooing of Olivia. Further examples of 'political' approaches to *Twelfth Night* include the following:

- Social hierarchy is established quickly through the use of titles such as 'Lord', and 'Lady'. The Captain calls Viola 'lady' and 'madam', and apologises for gossiping about his social superiors: 'What great ones do, the less will prattle of'. There are subtle reminders of different social rankings of characters throughout the play. For example, Feste (low social status) actively seeks tips, but Viola (high social status) indignantly dismisses Olivia's offered gratuity: 'I am no fee'd post, lady; keep your purse'.
- High-status characters are acutely conscious of the social position of themselves and others. Olivia's question 'What is your parentage?' suggests she wishes to assure herself that Cesario is of appropriate social status to be considered as a husband. Viola, disguised as Cesario, insists 'my state is well: / I am a gentleman'. Orsino assures Olivia of Sebastian's superior social rank: 'right noble is his blood'. Sir Toby expresses class-conscious contempt as Malvolio attempts to put a stop to midnight revelling: 'Art any more than a steward?' In the gulling scene, Sir Toby is incensed by Malvolio's fantasising about rising from the servant class to the ruling class (but it should be noted that some critics argue that Malvolio already has high social status by virtue of his important household function).

- The hierarchical nature of both Orsino's and Olivia's households implies acute gradations of social ranking. Stage productions often use 'business' and body language to suggest the class-conscious tensions and jealousies that exist between Orsino's courtiers. They are sometimes portrayed as clearly resenting Cesario's rapid promotion to the Duke's favour. In Olivia's household, Maria has been interpreted, like Malvolio, as a social climber, desperate to achieve higher class status (but she may already be from the gentry class, like many such 'gentlewomen' in Tudor households, even though the play never shows her in an intimate relationship with Olivia).

- Feste has been seen as excessively concerned about losing his employment. His anxiety has been claimed to echo the bleak economic insecurity of the servant class in Elizabethan England. Stage productions occasionally portray him as out of a job at the play's end, his melancholy increased by the uncertain future he now faces.

- Aspects of the play have been interpreted as covert criticism of the Elizabethan nobility. Sir Toby's cruelty towards Malvolio, and his exploitation of Sir Andrew is seen as typically callous aristocratic behaviour: uncaring towards social inferiors, and determined to profit from any weakness of his equals. Similarly, Sir Toby's foolishness has sometimes been interpreted as representative of his class. The self-indulgence of Orsino and Olivia is claimed as evidence of a privileged class which licenses its members to believe that only their own emotions are important.

- In Shakespeare's time, the word 'puritan' possessed not only religious but political meanings. It was used in that political sense by King James I to condemn opposition to his authority. From this perspective, Malvolio's meanness of spirit has been interpreted as representative of an emerging self-made class. Impatient with the old order, and intolerant of fun and festivity, new groupings of socially mobile men sought to take over the power traditionally exercised by the aristocratic class. Contemporary audiences' enjoyment of Malvolio's humiliation is interpreted as mocking, thus acting to defuse the threat that such a challenge to traditional authority represents. The Malvolio subplot has sometimes been suggested to foreshadow the class struggle to come in the English Civil War which began in 1642.

Paradoxically, the result of such 'political' interpretations often serves to heighten the importance of characters. They appear as isolated, each seeking their own advantage, and unconcerned for others. As such, they contradict notions of belonging to a community, but appear more as competitive products of a hierarchical, unequal society.

Two well-known critics who are often called upon in support of political interpretations are Jan Kott and Mikhail Bakhtin. The Polish critic Jan Kott fought with the Polish army and underground movement against the Nazis in the Second World War (1939–45), and had direct experience of the suffering and terror caused by Stalinist repression in Poland in the years after the war. Kott's book *Shakespeare our Contemporary* saw parallels between the violence and cruelty of the modern world and the worlds of tyranny and despair that Shakespeare depicted in his tragedies. Kott's discussion of *Twelfth Night* seems more concerned with sex than politics ('the real theme of Illyria, erotic delirium or the metamorphoses of sex'), but his judgement on the play, significantly contained in a chapter titled 'Shakespeare's bitter Arcadia', acerbically condemns its social world as a reflection of Elizabethan aristocratic self-centred hedonism:

> With all its appearances of gaiety, it is a very bitter comedy about the Elizabethan *dolce vita*

The Russian formalist Mikhail Bakhtin is best known for his concept of 'Carnival', the spirit of collective misrule (a notion similar to the assumptions of C L Barber, see page 87). Modern critics typically use Bakhtin to argue that the Elizabethan authorities used the licensed foolery of carnival as an instrument of social control. They permitted 'allowed licence' in order to effectively redirect and defuse subversive challenges to established power structures. In times of carnival (like the Twelfth Night festivities) dissident social energies could be released, and the powerful could be imitated and mocked, but the real conditions of power remained unchanged. Bakhtin's theory is evident in Michael Bristol's essay, which sees the process

> fully played out in Twelfth Night, as Carnival misrule in the persons of Toby and his companions . . . contends with Lent in the person of Malvolio.

Bristol argues that such battles are over the issue of 'political succession'. But he concludes that such struggles are never ended, either in *Twelfth Night* or in the real world:

> The battle of angry Carnival and sullen, vindictive Lent is not concluded in the represented world of Illyria, nor is it ever concluded in the world offstage.

Feminist criticism

Feminism aims to achieve rights and equality for women in social, political and economic life. It challenges sexism: those beliefs and practices which result in the degradation, oppression and subordination of women. Feminist critics therefore reject 'male ownership' of criticism in which men determined what questions were to be asked of a play, and which answers were acceptable. They argue that male criticism often neglects, represses or misrepresents female experience, and stereotypes or distorts women's points of view. Feminist criticism, like any 'approach', takes a wide variety of forms. Nonetheless, it is possible to identify certain major concerns for feminist critical writing on *Twelfth Night*.

Shakespeare's comedies hold special interest for feminist critics. Unlike the tragedies or histories, women characters have the major parts, and speak as many words as men. Their actions powerfully influence or direct the development of plot, they are witty and intelligent, more than holding their own with men in dialogue. Some, like Viola, are independent spirits, free to act in their dramatic worlds, apparently unshackled by father, husband or lover. A few female characters (Rosalind in *As You Like It*, Julia in *The Two Gentlemen of Verona*, and Viola) adopt male disguise to achieve their purposes. For feminist critics, such cross-dressing and gender ambiguity (and the fact that in Elizabethan times female roles were played by males) raise important questions of sexual politics and gender construction.

Feminists identify the many assumptions about gender in *Twelfth Night*. For example, Orsino claims that men and women are fundamentally different, but makes two quite different claims about that difference (see Act 2 Scene 4, lines 30–3, 89–95). Viola also suggests a range of differences: that women are easily moved, have waxen hearts, frailty, but that they are also similar to men ('true of heart as we'), and even more faithful (see Act 2 Scene 4, lines 112–14). Other gender assumptions and stereotypes include:

- the comic duel of Act 3 (only men can fight, and must do so for honour);
- references to the impermanence of women's beauty ('For women are as roses, whose fair flower, / Being once displayed, doth fall that very hour', Act 2 Scene 4, lines 36–7);
- that to have no children makes for a life without significance (see Viola's 'cruell'st she' speech, Act 1 Scene 5, lines 197–9, and as implied in Feste's 'O mistress mine' song in Act 2 Scene 3). Some feminists remark that this assumption is little more than a conventional male device to get women to agree to sex.

A major question for feminist criticism is whether Shakespeare's female characters confirm or subvert negative stereotypes of women as weak, submissive and pliable. Most feminists argue that *Twelfth Night* challenges such stereotyping, and shows in the characters of Viola and Olivia that it can be transcended. Feminists commonly approach a Shakespeare play using the notion of patriarchy (male domination of women). They point to the fact that throughout much of history power has been in the hands of men, both in society and in the family. But in *Twelfth Night* both Viola and Olivia escape patriarchal control and transcend the restrictions of social codes (indeed, the critic Leonard Tennenhouse asserts that *Twelfth Night* makes explicit 'the transfer of patriarchal power to a woman'). Both women show they can do much more than survive. Olivia is clearly in charge of her household, and Viola is not evidently constrained by father or brother. She is usually judged to defy the stereotype, her quick-wittedness and liveliness standing in dynamic contrast to Orsino's self-indulgent languor.

Some feminists, however, argue that in *Twelfth Night* negative stereotyping of women is not subverted. Viola, for all her clear-sightedness, falls head over heels for Orsino. Her love seems to make her blind to the less attractive side of his nature. Further, she is not an active agent for change in the play, but patiently decides to see how matters develop. Jean Howard, for example, is critical of how the play presents both Viola and Olivia, seeing both women ending up as subject to conventional male dominance in the hierarchy of marriage:

> The play disciplines independent women like Olivia . . . and
> rewards the self-abnegation of Viola.

An even more critical feminist interpretation of *Twelfth Night* is
Dympna Callaghan's contentious judgement that the Malvolio gulling
scene portrays the 'social enactment of women's oppression'. She
takes Malvolio's comment on the letter's handwriting 'and thus she
makes her great Ps' as an indication of female degradation:

> The allusion to Olivia's copious urination further deforms
> veiled, cloistered, aristocratic femininity into the grotesque,
> and, paradoxically, more suitable object of Malvolio's sexual
> and social ambitions.

Feminist criticism draws attention to other episodes and language
that are often overlooked or played down by many male critics.
Examples include:

- Antonio's strong desire leads him to follow Sebastian, which mirrors
  Olivia's pursuit of Cesario. Both transgress patriarchal convention
  which forbade both homosexuality and women taking the lead in
  courtship. Olivia is aware that her pursuit of Cesario oversteps the
  rules of conduct for a woman of her class ('Have you not set mine
  honour at the stake'). She runs the danger of social disgrace
  because social convention forbids the woman to take the lead in
  wooing. But her actions show she rejects such social restriction.
- Viola's cross-dressing enhanced erotic effect on Elizabethan
  audiences and opened up alternatives to the conventional view that
  marriage is a natural and desired outcome of comedy (and of real
  life). Some feminist readings claim that when Orsino declares
  Viola his 'fancy's queen' at the end of the play, what male
  spectators saw and responded to was the sight of two men holding
  hands. Such an interpretation challenges conventional views of
  love, and admits the possibility of other relationships.
- Viola's silence throughout the closing 100 lines of dialogue is
  usually interpreted as her consent to future marriage. In sharp
  contrast, some feminists interpret it as evidence of the reduction of
  women's status. They claim it shows that even such a feisty
  character as Viola can only submit to male desire and dominance.

- The play is remarkable for its 'absent mothers'. Olivia is in thrall to her dead father and brother, and Viola's father has both mention and significance, but there is no mention of Olivia's or Viola's mother. Such absence (common in other Shakespeare plays) reveals much about the lower status of women in Elizabethan England.

Such readings (like all critical interpretations) raise the question of whether they are what Shakespeare intended. Was he purposefully challenging female stereotyping, or official condemnation of homosexuality? Whilst many critics today argue that Shakespeare's intentions can never be known, a distinctive feature of feminist criticism is to suggest that *Twelfth Night* and the other comedies subject patriarchal conventions to critical scrutiny, exposing them as irrational and repressive. The implication is that *Twelfth Night* shows that love can be a partnership of equals, and that women's desires and capacity for feeling are on equal terms with men's, not inferior to them. In *Twelfth Night*, as in all his comedies, Shakespeare portrays intelligent and spirited women who more than hold their own in the love battles of the sexes.

Performance criticism

Performance criticism fully acknowledges that *Twelfth Night* is a play: a script to be performed by actors to an audience. It examines all aspects of the play in performance: its staging in the theatre or on film and video. Performance criticism focuses on Shakespeare's stagecraft and the semiotics of theatre (signs: words, costumes, gestures, etc.), together with the 'afterlife' of the play (what happened to *Twelfth Night* after Shakespeare wrote it). That involves scrutiny of how productions at different periods have presented the play. As such, performance criticism appraises how the text has been cut, added to, rewritten and rearranged to present a version felt appropriate to the times.

The early popularity of the play has been commented on above (page 81), but it seems that soon after Samuel Pepys saw three productions in the 1660s it fell from favour for around 80 years. Nonetheless, other playwrights drew upon it as a resource for ideas and language. For example, William Wycherley used aspects of *Twelfth Night* in his play *The Plain Dealer*, 1676. Wycherley's main character, like Orsino, suffers from unrequited love, and is loved in turn by the Viola-like character disguised as his page. A different adaptation, sticking more closely to the plot, appeared in 1703 in William Burnaby's *Love Betray'd* in which Olivia displays the cynical wit of Restoration Comedy heroines.

Such adaptations seem to have been preferred until 1741. In that year, at London's Drury Lane Theatre, Charles Macklin restored *Twelfth Night* to popularity. Macklin's successful playing of Malvolio set a fashion for major actors to play the role. Although much of Shakespeare's own play was now performed, productions added all kinds of 'improvements'. In 1820, an operatic version included no fewer than 16 songs and sonnets.

Throughout the nineteenth century, productions of *Twelfth Night* increasingly seized every opportunity for spectacle and music. The 'festive' aspect of the play was often taken very literally to present all kinds of merriment and revelling. A production in 1894 included two shipwreck scenes, and opened with fishermen and peasants on a beach singing 'Come unto these yellow sands' from *The Tempest*. In another, Orsino and Viola married in grand style in Illyria's cathedral. Sets became very elaborate, featuring fountains, staircases, grassy terraces and grand country house interiors, as designers attempted to portray 'realistic' versions of Illyria (which in practice usually meant Victorian conceptions of a mythical Elizabethan 'Merry England').

Among such spectacles, Malvolio was often portrayed as a ridiculous figure. In one production four miniature Malvolios followed a patently vain and vacuous Malvolio whose pomposity was not punctured even when he fell down a staircase. But, in what is often considered a landmark performance, Sir Henry Irving presented a 'gaunt and sombre steward', a tragic figure whose imprisonment was evidently intended to evoke audience sympathy and pity. Irving's influential portrayal is often claimed to be influenced by Lamb's conception of Malvolio's gravity and dignity (see page 83).

The twentieth century saw a return to much simpler stagings of the play. Although the tradition of extravagant productions lingered on, most productions no longer attempted to create an impression of realism. Under the influence of William Poel and Harley Granville Barker, the stage was cleared of the clutter of historical detail. The aim was to recapture the conditions of the Elizabethan bare stage, which was not dependent on theatrical illusion. That implied a minimum of scenery, scenes flowing swiftly into each other, and a concern for clear speaking of Shakespeare's language.

Space makes it impossible to detail the great variety of ways in which *Twelfth Night* has been performed throughout the twentieth and into the twenty-first century. But two generalisations can be made, one about mood, the other about character. Both illustrate how criticism and stage performance have mutually influenced each other.

Productions have increasingly attempted to bring out the complex variety of moods in the play, but with a concern to portray its autumnal, elegiac qualities, suggesting that fertility and romantic idyll will soon give way to decay and winter. Such stagings reflect critical writing about Shakespeare's development as a dramatist. The argument goes that *Twelfth Night* was Shakespeare's 'farewell to comedy'. Written around 1601 (see page 57), it ended the sequence that included such comedies as *A Midsummer Night's Dream*, *Much Ado About Nothing* and *As You Like It*. His mind was now turning to the tragedies: *Hamlet* was probably written around the same time as *Twelfth Night*, and other great tragedies lay ahead.

This perspective of Shakespeare's playwriting career encourages some critics to see him rejecting romance and mirth, and casting shadows over the revels of the play. They point out that the play contains no romantic courtship dialogue between Orsino and Viola, or between Olivia and Sebastian, and they detect darker strains in *Twelfth Night* which foreshadow the tragedies to come. Greater stress is placed on the troubling possibilities of the play, the sense of melancholy, the awareness of mortality. The perception of *Twelfth Night* is no longer that of a romantic comedy with strong elements of farce, but of a much more complex, painful drama. An early expression of this harsher view is by the poet W H Auden:

> Shakespeare was in no mood for comedy, but in a mood of puritanical aversion to all those pleasing illusions which men cherish and by which they lead their lives

In the same vein, Ralph Berry also speculates that at the end of *Twelfth Night* Shakespeare demolishes its festive mood:

> The Illyrian world of fulfilled romance, genial comics, and harmless pranks metamorphoses into an image of the real

world, with its grainy texture, social frictions, and real pain inflicted upon real people.

The complexity of the moods of the play is mirrored in complexity of characterisation. Malvolio is no longer seen as simply a figure of fun who fully deserves his cruel humiliation, but as a character who invites a complicated, ambiguous audience response. John Russell Brown's comments admirably suggest the variety of ways in which other characters can, and have been, portrayed:

> Feste, the fool, can be melancholy, or bitter, or professional or amorous (and sometimes impressively silent), or self-contained and philosophical, or bawdy and impotent. Sir Andrew Aguecheek can be patient, sunny, feckless, gormless, animated or neurotic . . . Orsino can be mature or very young; poetic; or weak; or strong but deceived; or real and distant. The text can suggest a Viola who is pert, sentimental, lyrical, practical, courageous or helpless. Shakespeare's words can support all these interpretations, and others; there are few plays which give comparable scope for enterprise and originality. The characters, the situations and the speeches are protean.

Performance criticism also stresses that *Twelfth Night* contains much evidence of Shakespeare's interest in the theatre. There is much use of the language of drama: Olivia asks Cesario 'Are you a comedian?' and words from theatrical practice recur: 'speech', 'part', 'con' (learn a part), 'play'. Throughout the play, Shakespeare keeps the audience humorously aware of both their own real world and the fictional stage world, most notably in Fabian's remark:

> If this were played upon a stage now, I could condemn it as an
> improbable fiction.   *(Act 3 Scene 4, lines 108–9)*

Here Shakespeare acknowledges the audience, makes them complicit in the enjoyment of the fiction, but also reminds them that behind the illusion of Illyria is the artifice of his dramatic skill. The same qualities can be seen as Feste switches roles to play Sir Topas, leaves Malvolio with a song about the 'old Vice' (a stock character of morality plays), and in the closing words of his final song as he acknowledges the audience, 'And we'll strive to please you every day'. At such moments, as a play that stresses its own theatricality it becomes what is referred to today as 'metatheatre': theatre about theatre.

Psychoanalytic criticism

In the twentieth century, psychoanalysis became a major influence on the understanding and interpretation of human behaviour. The founder of psychoanalysis, Sigmund Freud, explained personality as the result of unconscious and irrational desires, repressed memories or wishes, sexuality, fantasy, anxiety and conflict. Freud's theories have had a strong influence on criticism and stagings of Shakespeare's plays, most obviously on *Hamlet* in the well-known claim that Hamlet suffers from an Oedipus complex.

Twelfth Night has attracted comparatively little psychoanalytic critical writing. As Norman Holland points out, such critics usually discuss the play through analysis of characters. Holland's book, *Psychoanalysis and Shakespeare*, details the major features of such psychoanalytic interpretations:

- Malvolio seems a narcissist ('sick of self-love'), but actually suffers from lack of love for himself. He is the superego of the play: a kind of punishing 'policeman'. He not only tries to repress pleasure in others; he denies his own natural desires. His attempts to impose strict rule on Olivia's household reveal that he secretly feels inferior, and possesses self-hatred.
- Characters use fantasies to protect themselves. Orsino refuses to grow up, using 'shadow love' for Olivia to deny himself real love. Olivia uses mourning for her brother as a similar defence mechanism. Malvolio's fantasies compensate for his lack of power.
- Orsino is fixated on Olivia as a mother substitute (older and unavailable).
- Olivia is frigid. Her brother, older than she, dominated her, causing her to develop a taboo: rejecting men holding power. Because the disguised Viola is young and powerless, the taboo does not inhibit Olivia's desire.

Such interpretations fail to give a coherent view of the whole play. They reveal the obvious weaknesses in applying psychoanalytic theories to *Twelfth Night*. They are highly speculative, and can be neither proved nor disproved, Psychoanalytic approaches are therefore often accused of imposing interpretations based on theory rather than upon Shakespeare's text. Nonetheless, the play has obvious features which seem to invite psychoanalytic approaches: Illyria's association with fantasy and imagination, instability of language, disguise and mistaken identity, and the emotional preoccupation with love, hedonistic enjoyment and melancholy.

Postmodern criticism

Postmodern criticism (sometimes called 'deconstruction') is not always easy to understand because it is not centrally concerned with consistency or reasoned argument. It does not accept that one section of the story is necessarily connected to what follows, or that characters relate to each other in meaningful ways. Because of such assumptions, postmodern criticism is sometimes described as 'reading against the grain' or less politely as 'textual harassment'. The approach therefore has obvious drawbacks in providing a model for examination students who are expected to display reasoned, coherent argument, and respect for the evidence of the text.

Postmodernism often revels in the cleverness of its own use of language, and accepts all kinds of anomalies and contradictions in a spirit of playfulness or 'carnival'. It abandons any notion of the organic unity of the play, and rejects the assumption that a Shakespeare play possesses clear patterns or themes. Some postmodern critics even deny the possibility of finding meaning in language. They claim that words simply refer to other words, and so any interpretation is endlessly delayed (or 'deferred' as the deconstructionists say). Others focus on minor or marginal characters, or on loose ends, gaps or silences in the play, claiming that these features, often overlooked as unimportant, reveal significant truths about the play.

Postmodern approaches to *Twelfth Night* are most clearly seen in stage productions. There, you could think of it as simply 'a mixture of styles'. The label 'postmodern' is applied to productions which self-consciously show little regard for consistency in character, or for coherence in telling the story. Characters are dressed in costumes from very different historical periods, and carry both modern and ancient weapons. Ironically, Shakespeare himself has been regarded as a postmodern writer in the way he mixes genres in his plays, comedy with tragedy.

Geoffrey Hartman provides a succinct deconstructive account of how traditional criticism reveals more about critics themselves than about Shakespeare's text. Hartman's claim that criticism should focus on language ('in literature, everything aspires to the condition of language') is typical of postmodern critics who make much of the instability of language. In practice, this often means little more than traditional notions of ambiguity: that words can have different meanings. It has long been accepted that Shakespeare's language has multiple, not single meanings. In *Twelfth Night*, that openness to multiple meanings is evident, but it is expressed by Terry Eagleton in what some judge the typically excessive and self-referential language of postmodernism:

> If desire tends to overwhelm any determinate signified or stable meaning with an excess of signifiers, then it is appropriate that Orsino at the opening of *Twelfth Night* should link it to music, an art form of the signifier alone, and one of which he wishes to surfeit and die. *Twelfth Night* is fascinated by the idea of words being torn from their material contexts to become self-generating, a tangled chain of metaphor which nowhere seems to button down on reality.

Organising your responses

The purpose of this section is to help you improve your writing about *Twelfth Night*. It offers practical guidance on two kinds of tasks: writing about an extract from the play and writing an essay. Whether you are answering an examination question, preparing coursework (term papers), or carrying out research into your own chosen topic, this section will help you organise and present your responses.

In all your writing, there are three vital things to remember:

- *Twelfth Night* is a play. Although it is usually referred to as a 'text', *Twelfth Night* is not a book, but a script intended to be acted on a stage. So your writing should demonstrate an awareness of the play in performance as theatre. That means you should always try to read the play with an 'inner eye', thinking about how it could look and sound on stage. The next best thing to seeing an actual production is to imagine yourself sitting in the audience, watching and listening to *Twelfth Night* being performed. By doing so, you will be able to write effectively about Shakespeare's language and dramatic techniques.

- *Twelfth Night* is not a presentation of 'reality'. It is a dramatic construct in which the playwright, through theatre, engages the emotions and intellect of the audience. The characters and story may persuade an audience to suspend its disbelief for several hours. The audience may identify with the characters, be deeply moved by them, and may think of them as if they are living human beings. However, when you write, a major part of your task is to show how Shakespeare achieves his dramatic effects that so engage the audience. Through discussion of his handling of language, character and plot, your writing reveals how Shakespeare uses themes and ideas, attitudes and values, to give insight into crucial social, moral and political dilemmas of his time – and yours.

- How Shakespeare learned his craft. As a schoolboy, and in his early years as a dramatist, Shakespeare used all kinds of models or frameworks to guide his writing. But he quickly learned how to vary and adapt the models to his own dramatic purposes. This section offers frameworks that you can use to structure your writing. As you use them, follow Shakespeare's example! Adapt them to suit your own writing style and needs.

Writing about an extract

It is an expected part of all Shakespeare study that you should be able to write well about an extract (sometimes called a 'passage') from the play. An extract is usually between 30 to 70 lines long, and you are invited to comment on it. The instructions vary. Sometimes the task is very briefly expressed:

- Write a detailed commentary on the following passage.
- Write about the effect of the extract on your own thoughts and feelings.

At other times a particular focus is specified for your writing:

- With close reference to the language and imagery of the passage, show in what ways it helps to establish important issues in the play.
- Analyse the style and structure of the extract, showing what it contributes to your appreciation of the play's major concerns.

In writing your response, you must of course take account of the precise wording of the task, and ensure you concentrate on each particular point specified. But however the invitation to write about an extract is expressed, it requires you to comment in detail on the language. You should identify and evaluate how the language reveals character, contributes to plot development, offers opportunities for dramatic effect, and embodies crucial concerns of the play as a whole. These 'crucial concerns' are also referred to as the 'themes', or 'issues', or 'preoccupations' of the play.

The following framework is a guide to how you can write a detailed commentary on an extract. Writing a paragraph on each item will help you bring out the meaning and significance of the extract, and show how Shakespeare achieves his effects.

> **Paragraph 1:** Locate the extract in the play and say who is on stage.
>
> **Paragraph 2:** State what the extract is about and identify its structure.
>
> **Paragraph 3:** Identify the mood or atmosphere of the extract.
>
> **Paragraphs 4–8:**
>   Diction (vocabulary)
>   Imagery
>   Antithesis
>   Repetition
>   Lists
> These paragraphs analyse how Shakespeare achieves his effects. They concentrate on the language of the extract, showing the dramatic effect of each item, and how the language expresses crucial concerns of the play.
>
> **Paragraph 9:** Staging opportunities
>
> **Paragraph 10:** Conclusion

The following example uses the framework to show how the paragraphs making up the essay might be written. The framework headings (in bold), would not of course appear in your essay. They are presented only to help you see how the framework is used.

Extract

OLIVIA   What is your name?

VIOLA   Cesario is your servant's name, fair princess.

OLIVIA   My servant, sir? 'Twas never merry world
       Since lowly feigning was called compliment.
       Y'are servant to the Count Orsino, youth.   5

VIOLA   And he is yours, and his must needs be yours:
       Your servant's servant is your servant, madam.

OLIVIA   For him, I think not on him; for his thoughts,
       Would they were blanks, rather than filled with me!

VIOLA   Madam, I come to whet your gentle thoughts   10
       On his behalf.

OLIVIA   O by your leave, I pray you!
       I bade you never speak again of him;
       But would you undertake another suit
       I had rather hear you to solicit that,
       Than music from the spheres.

VIOLA   Dear lady –   15

OLIVIA   Give me leave, beseech you. I did send,
       After the last enchantment you did here,
       A ring in chase of you. So did I abuse

Myself, my servant, and, I fear me, you.
Under your hard construction must I sit, 20
To force that on you in a shameful cunning
Which you knew none of yours. What might you think?
Have you not set mine honour at the stake,
And baited it with all th'unmuzzled thoughts
That tyrannous heart can think? To one of your receiving 25
Enough is shown; a cypress, not a bosom,
Hides my heart: so, let me hear you speak.

VIOLA   I pity you.

OLIVIA   That's a degree to love.

VIOLA   No, not a grise; for 'tis a vulgar proof
That very oft we pity enemies. 30

OLIVIA   Why then, methinks 'tis time to smile again.
O world, how apt the poor are to be proud!
If one should be a prey, how much the better
To fall before the lion than the wolf!

[Clock strikes]

The clock upbraids me with the waste of time. 35
Be not afraid, good youth; I will not have you –
And yet when wit and youth is come to harvest,
Your wife is like to reap a proper man.
There lies your way, due west.

VIOLA   Then westward ho!
Grace and good disposition attend your ladyship! 40
You'll nothing, madam, to my lord by me?

OLIVIA   Stay!
I prithee tell me what thou think'st of me.

VIOLA   That you do think you are not what you are.

OLIVIA   If I think so, I think the same of you. 45

VIOLA   Then think you right: I am not what I am.

OLIVIA   I would you were as I would have you be.

VIOLA   Would it be better, madam, than I am?
I wish it might, for now I am your fool.

OLIVIA   *[Aside]* O what a deal of scorn looks beautiful 50
In the contempt and anger of his lip!
A murd'rous guilt shows not itself more soon,
Than love that would seem hid. Love's night is noon.
Cesario, by the roses of the spring,

>   By maidhood, honour, truth, and everything,   55
>   I love thee so that, maugre all thy pride,
>   Nor wit nor reason can my passion hide.
>   Do not extort thy reasons from this clause,
>   For that I woo, thou therefore hast no cause;
>   But rather reason thus with reason fetter: 60
>   Love sought is good, but giv'n unsought is better.
> VIOLA   By innocence I swear, and by my youth,
>   I have one heart, one bosom, and one truth,
>   And that no woman has; nor never none
>   Shall mistress be of it, save I alone.   65
>   And so, adieu, good madam; never more
>   Will I my master's tears to you deplore.
> OLIVIA   Yet come again: for thou perhaps mayst move
>   That heart which now abhors to like his love.

(Act 3 Scene 1, lines 81–149)

Paragraph 1: Locate the extract in the play and identify who is on stage.
Viola, disguised as Cesario, has returned to Olivia to bring a further
message of love to her from Orsino. At their previous meeting, Olivia
fell in love with the disguised Viola, and resorted to a trick of sending
a ring to ensure that 'he' returns. Viola has seen through the trick and
knows that Olivia has mistaken her for a man. Olivia has just dismissed
Sir Toby and Sir Andrew, and is now alone on stage with Viola.

Paragraph 2: State what the extract is about and identify its structure.
(Begin with one or two sentences identifying what the extract is about,
followed by several sentences briefly identifying its structure, that is,
the unfolding events and the different sections of the extract.)

The extract shows Olivia refusing to hear further messages of love
from Orsino, and revealing her love for Cesario (the disguised Viola).
It begins with Viola attempting to speak for Orsino, but Olivia
refusing to listen and hinting she would rather hear Cesario's own
declaration of love for her. She admits the trick of the ring, and
declares her feelings are clearly evident. She seems to dismiss Viola,
but then calls her back, and in their exchange Viola hints at her true
identity: 'I am not what I am'. Olivia unambiguously declares her love,
and uses logic to justify why Viola should accept it. But Viola swears
no woman except herself shall ever have her heart.

Paragraph 3: Identify the mood or atmosphere of the extract.

Olivia wishes to create a mood of love, but the entire extract is full of dramatic irony. The audience and Viola know what Olivia does not. Mistaking Viola's disguise, she thinks Cesario is male. The irony affects each one of Olivia's moods as she successively flirts, begs, seems to blame Cesario for cruelty in love, then seems to give up any claim to 'him', only to make up her mind to passionately declare her love. The dramatic irony creates both humour and poignancy through Olivia's mistaking and Viola's responses which the audience, but not Olivia, understands.

Paragraph 4: Diction (vocabulary)

Olivia unconsciously gives a clue to the dramatic irony that pervades the extract when she accuses Viola of 'lowly feigning': pretended humility. Viola is feigning, but not in the way Olivia thinks. Viola's language seems clear, and is usually less elaborate than Olivia's, but within its seeming clarity lies the ambiguity that comes from her disguise. Several words present difficulties for modern audiences because they have dropped out of use: 'blanks' (empty sheets of paper), 'cypress' (thin linen), 'grise' (step), 'maugre' (in spite of). For Elizabethans, each word was contextually appropriate; today their very unfamiliarity can add to the strangely ambiguous climate of the episode. Most importantly, however, Olivia switches from 'you' to 'thee' and 'thou' as she declares her love. The change had great significance for Elizabethans, because 'thou' could imply a close emotional attachment that was not present in 'you'.

Paragraph 5: Imagery

Olivia uses a rich variety of images to express the strength of her passion for Cesario. She would rather hear Cesario declare his love 'Than music from the spheres': the wonderfully harmonious music Elizabethans believed the planets created as they revolved in concentric crystal spheres. She accuses Cesario of 'enchantment', and uses an image of bear-baiting to blame 'him' of cruelty as she compares herself to a bear, tied to a stake, attacked by unmuzzled dogs. The painful image suggests her agony, but feels rather excessive and self-pitying. So too does her comparison of Viola to a beast of prey, a wolf or even a lion. She uses a gentler image from the Elizabethan countryside when she speaks of Cesario's future wife reaping at 'harvest' a proper man. When she finally decides to declare her love, Olivia uses two images to assert that truth will always emerge. One is surprisingly from crime: 'murd'rous guilt' cannot be hidden. The second is from the tradition of romance: 'Love's night is noon'. Both striking images express the extreme and romantic nature of her feelings. Elsewhere in the extract, briefer images enrich meaning and emotional effect: Olivia's heart is hidden by only thin linen ('cypress'); Viola says she comes to sharpen ('whet') Olivia's thoughts for Orsino; 'heart' is used by both women to signify love.

Paragraph 6: Antithesis
Antithesis expresses conflict, and Shakespeare uses it in the extract to convey different kinds of oppositions. In the first playful exchange 'servant' is set against 'princess', 'feigning' against 'compliment' as Viola and Olivia attempt to establish or deny their relationship. Olivia rejects Orsino's 'love-thoughts' wishing they were 'blanks' rather than 'filled with [her]', but in her final line offers a promise of love in 'abhors' against 'like'. Close to expressing her love for Cesario, Olivia antithetically declares 'a cypress, not a bosom, / Hides my heart', and then self-pityingly thinks of herself as 'poor' to Viola's 'proud', and sets 'lion' against 'wolf'. She decides that her love cannot be hidden, 'Love's night is noon', and tries to persuade Viola that 'unsought' love is better than 'sought'. But the most striking antithesis is expressed in the simplest language, and catches the essence of the conflict between reality and appearance that runs through the entire play: 'I am not what I am'.

Paragraph 7: Repetition
Repetition of words, rhythms and sounds increase dramatic effect in different ways. The six repetitions of 'servant' in the opening exchange are playful, but Olivia's humorous uses of the word have a mocking edge. Similarly, her almost obsessive use of 'you' throughout the extract, although the pronoun conventionally implied a distant relationship, reveals clearly who is uppermost in her thoughts and feelings (actors sometimes heavily emphasise a 'you' to make those thoughts and feelings even more obvious). Viola's echo, 'Then westward ho!' had special appeal to Elizabethans who heard the Thames ferrymen call out the phrase near the Globe as they picked up passengers for Westminster. The extract contains subtle repetitions of

rhythm as each character speaks. That repetition is most obvious in the single-line, rapid-fire exchanges of lines 43–8 (known as *stichomythia*) in which almost every word is monosyllabic, adding to the forcefulness of the repeated rhythm. Shakespeare adds repetition of sound to rhythm as Olivia declares her love (lines 54–61). Both Olivia and Viola use rhyming couplets ('soon' / 'noon', 'spring' / 'everything' and so on to 'move' / 'love' – which rhymed in Shakespeare's day). The effect is to heighten the romantic, almost fairy-tale quality of what the characters say, appropriate to such a fanciful moment tinged with echoes of an older literary tradition of courtly love.

Paragraph 8: Lists

Shakespeare's fondness for piling up items, rather like a list, for different dramatic purposes is evident in the extract. Here, such lists tend to be short, only three items or so. Olivia itemises, with growing regret, whom she has deceived: 'Myself, my servant, and, I fear me, you'. She swears her love, listing what she holds most dear, with accumulating force, 'by the roses of the spring, / By maidhood, honour, truth, and everything'. But Viola, echoing her sworn oath, rejects her love, and emphatically implies her real identity behind another list that gains force from each repeated 'one': 'I have one heart, one bosom, and one truth'.

Paragraph 9: Staging opportunities

How the two characters behave towards each other on stage can take very different forms. But the language implies that Olivia takes the initiative throughout. It might be helpful for a director to think of the episode as a fencing match, with Olivia on the attack throughout, and Viola on the defensive, knowing she has to 'fight', but unwilling to wound, and wishing to escape. Viola can physically, but always courteously, attempt to keep her distance as Olivia with equal courtesy but evident emotion tries to establish physical contact as well as emotional closeness. That physical contact can be dramatically justified most appropriately as Olivia declares her love in lines 54–61. She can take Viola's hand, or perhaps touch her cheek. The inbuilt stage direction 'The clock upbraids me' offers Olivia an opportunity to display a major mood change as, briefly, she decides to give up her pursuit of Cesario. But within four lines, Shakespeare has her renewing her interest again as she asks Viola for her thoughts of her. In the following single-line exchanges the characters might be seen to echo each other's gestures and expressions to accompany their echoing words and rhythms.

Above all, the staging should attempt to bring out the dramatic irony, with Viola all too aware that Olivia is mistaken about her true identity, and increasingly concerned to extract herself from a difficult, sexually ambiguous situation. She can display evident relief on 'Then westward ho!', but it would ruin Shakespeare's sensitively constructed interaction between the characters if she were to overtly share her knowledge with the audience, for example by winking at them. However it is possible for Olivia to share her aside at lines 50–3 directly with the audience, and involve them in her decision to reveal her love.

Paragraph 10: Conclusion
The extract, with Olivia's open declaration of love, marks a significant turning point in the play. It compounds both the humour and the complexity of the action, leaving the audience wondering just how the love tangle can be resolved. The extract shows the development of Olivia's character. She has changed dramatically. All her earlier thoughts of mourning for seven years for her brother are abandoned. She is now in headlong pursuit of Cesario, at the end of the extract imploring him to return to her. Although Olivia is quite unlike Malvolio and Sir Andrew, Shakespeare shows that she, like them, is similarly afflicted by not being able to see things clearly. She too suffers from delusions of love, with comic and touching results. The extract also provides further insight into Viola's character, who uses simple language with grace, discretion and concern not to hurt the self-deluded Olivia. But perhaps most evidently, the scene displays Shakespeare's playwriting skill, showing how he uses language, situation and character to create pervasive dramatic irony, and to embody the play's central themes, notably disguise, mistaken identity and the resulting follies of love.

Reminders

- The framework is only a guide. It helps you to structure your writing. Use the framework for practice on other extracts. Adapt it as you feel appropriate. Make it your own.
- Structure your response in paragraphs. Each paragraph makes a particular point and helps build up your argument.
- Focus tightly on the language, especially vocabulary, imagery, antithesis, lists, repetitions.
- Remember that *Twelfth Night* is a play, a drama intended for performance. The purpose of writing about an extract is to identify how Shakespeare creates dramatic effect. What techniques does he use?
- Try to imagine the action. Visualise the scene in your mind's eye. But remember there can be many valid ways of performing a scene. Offer alternatives. Justify your own preferences by reference to the language.
- Who is on stage? Imagine their interaction. How do 'silent characters' react to what's said?
- Look for the theatrical qualities of the extract. What guides for actors' movements and expressions are given in the language? Comment on any stage directions.
- How might the audience respond? In Elizabethan times? Today? How might you respond as a member of the audience?
- How might the lines be spoken? Think about tone, emphasis, pace, pauses. Identify shifting moods and registers. Is the verse pattern smooth or broken; flowing or full of hesitations and abrupt turns?
- What is the importance of the extract in the play as a whole? Justify its thematic significance.
- Are there any 'key words'?
- How does the extract develop the plot, reveal character, deepen themes?
- Offer a variety of interpretations.
- Avoid expressions that use the second person plural ('We feel . . .', 'our sympathies . . .', etc.). Express your own response to the episode presented in the extract, and acknowledge that others may respond differently.

Writing an essay

As part of your study of *Twelfth Night* you will be asked to write essays, either under examination conditions or for coursework (term papers). Examinations mean that you are under pressure of time, usually having around one hour to prepare and write each essay. Coursework means that you have much longer to think about and produce your essay. But whatever the type of essay, each will require you to develop an argument about a particular aspect of *Twelfth Night*.

Before suggesting a strategy for your essay-writing, it is helpful to recall just what an essay is. 'Essay' comes from the French *essai*: to attempt, or to make a trial. It was originally used by the sixteenth-century French writer Montaigne (whose work Shakespeare certainly read). Montaigne used *essais* to attempt to find out what he thought about particular subjects, such as 'friendship', or 'cannibals' or 'education'. In each essay he used many practical examples to test his response to the topic.

The essays you write on *Twelfth Night* similarly require that you set out your thoughts on a particular aspect of the play, using evidence from the text. The people who read your essays (examiners, teachers, lecturers) will have certain expectations for your writing. In each essay they will expect you to discuss and analyse a particular topic, using evidence from the play to develop an argument in an organised, coherent and persuasive way. Examiners look for, and reward, what they call 'an informed personal response'. This simply means that you show you have good knowledge of the play ('informed') and can use evidence from it to support and justify your own viewpoint ('personal').

You can write about *Twelfth Night* from different points of view. As pages 89–103 show, you can approach the play from a number of critical perspectives (feminist, political, psychoanalytic, etc.). You can also set the play in its social, literary and other contexts, as shown in the section on Contexts. You should write at different levels, moving beyond description to analysis and evaluation. Simply telling the story or describing characters is not as effective as analysing how events or characters embody wider concerns of the play.

In *Twelfth Night*, these 'wider concerns' (also called themes, issues, preoccupations – or more simply 'what the play is about') include love, appearance and reality, mistaken identity, time, festivity and enjoyment ('carnival') versus restraint and sobriety ('puritanism'), friendship, Elizabethan England. In your writing, always give practical examples (quotations, actions) which illustrate the themes you discuss.

How should you answer an examination question or write a coursework essay? The following threefold structure can help you organise your response:

opening paragraph
developing paragraphs
concluding paragraph.

Opening paragraph. Begin with a paragraph identifying just what topic or issue you will focus on. Show that you have understood what the question is about. You probably will have prepared for particular topics. But look closely at the question and identify key words to see what particular aspect it asks you to write about. Adapt your material to answer that question. Examiners do not reward an essay, however well written, if it is not on the question set.

Developing paragraphs. This is the main body of your essay. In it, you develop your argument, point by point, paragraph by paragraph. Use evidence from the play that illuminates the topic or issue, and answers the question set. Each paragraph makes a point of dramatic or thematic significance. Some paragraphs could make points concerned with context or particular critical approaches. The effect of your argument builds up as each paragraph adds to the persuasive quality of your essay. Use brief quotations that support your argument, and show clearly just why they are relevant. Ensure that your essay demonstrates that you are aware that *Twelfth Night* is a play; a drama intended for performance, and therefore open to a wide variety of interpretations and audience response. Remember to avoid the use of 'we' and 'our' ('We feel . . .', 'our sympathies . . .', etc.), and don't be afraid to be critical of writing that uses such expressions.

Concluding paragraph. Your final paragraph pulls together your main conclusions. It does not simply repeat what you have written earlier, but summarises concisely how your essay has successfully answered the question.

Example

> Question: In what ways do you consider *Twelfth Night* to be more than simply an entertaining comedy?

The following notes show the 'ingredients' of an answer. In an examination it is usually helpful to prepare similar notes from which you write your essay, paragraph by paragraph. Remember that examiners are not impressed by 'name-dropping': use of critics' names. What they want you to show is your own knowledge and judgement of the play and its contexts, and your understanding of how it has been interpreted from different critical perspectives.

Opening paragraph

Show that you are aware that the question asks you to show your understanding of *Twelfth Night* as 'simply an entertaining comedy', and then to give reasons for how far you judge the play to be more than that description. So include the following points and aim to write a sentence or more on each:

- Interpreting the play as 'simply an entertaining comedy' implies an approach which sees it as merely an amusing and charming play, sunny and always enjoyable.
- Filled with innocent laughter and preposterous situations, it has a happy ending which restores harmony to the temporary confusion of Illyria.
- All the characters are likeable and funny: Sir Toby is a lovable rogue, and even Malvolio has comic appeal, especially when he gets what he deserves at the play's end.
- From this perspective, the whole play is simply a delightful entertainment which must never be taken seriously. It is simply good for two to three hours' laughter in the theatre.
- But this is a stereotypical traditional approach which fails to recognise other valid interpretations and approaches that the complexity of the play invites.

Developing paragraphs

Now write a paragraph on each of a number of different ways in which the play might be interpreted both on stage and in criticism. In each paragraph, identify particular examples of the approaches you discuss. Some of the points you might include are given briefly below.

A play about different types of love
- The play is about love in its many forms, but with true love winning through at the end.
- Olivia and Orsino are the mourning lady and romantic hero of literary convention (expressed in such overblown language as 'Love-thoughts lie rich when canopied with bowers'). Their selfish, self-centred infatuations are transformed to genuine love by the constancy, integrity and clear-headedness of Viola, who embodies true and faithful love.
- Even Sir Toby finds a kind of love with Maria.
- Sir Andrew and Malvolio learn that playing at love, or self-love, is not enough.

A poignant, elegiac play
- The play is wistful and sentimental. The humour, apart from Sir Toby's coarseness, is witty and tender.
- There are many moving moments, for example as Viola speaks her beautiful and poignant lines of love in Act 1 Scene 5 ('Hallow your name to the reverberate hills'). She longs for a fulfilment, which, until the end of the play, is out of her grasp.
- The elegiac note is struck constantly with the many references to time ('Youth's a stuff will not endure'), and in the reminders of the ever-changing sea that echo through the play.
- Feste's songs are reminders that love, like life, will end.

A play with troubling undertones
- An upsetting play that seems to be light and amusing on the surface, but has dark and harsh depths.
- It is an uneasy play about outsiders who lose. Antonio is left sad and alone at the end. Malvolio leaves seeking revenge, not reconciliation ('I'll be revenged on the whole pack of you!').
- Orsino and Olivia are smug and self-centred. They learn nothing, and are just the same at the end of the play as at the beginning.
- Illyria is an oppressive society where no one at the top works. It breeds self-indulgent, idle aristocrats.

- Maria and her fellow-conspirators are prompted by ill-will towards Malvolio. The cruel baiting of Malvolio is theatre as blood sport.
- Malvolio is a scapegoat, because Illyria needs him as someone to punish for the misdeeds of society.
- The play is a cruel satire which contains signs that Shakespeare's dramatic thoughts were turning towards tragedy.
- The play foreshadows the English Civil War, the triumph of the puritans and the extinguishing of theatre and merriment.

An elusive play
- *Twelfth Night* is like quicksilver, elusive and impossible to grasp. It is always taking different shapes and meanings. A strange mixture, sometimes funny, sometimes sad.
- It is a kaleidoscope of characters and events, all with mysterious sides to them.
- It contains both romance and revenge, and it is open to interpretation whether love really triumphs, or whether revenge and uncertainty will follow.

An actor's play (metatheatre)
- *Twelfth Night* is a play which revels in its own theatricality, most obviously in Fabian's remark 'If this were played upon a stage now, I could condemn it as an improbable fiction.'
- It delights in disguise, double-dealing, wordplay and illusion. Viola acts the part of a boy; Malvolio acts the part of a deluded lover.
- It presents opportunities for actors to explore the slipperiness of language, and the dramatic irony which arises from disguise and mistaken identity.

Concluding paragraph
Write several sentences pulling together your conclusions. You might include the following points:

- The play raises crucial questions about different kinds of love (e.g. Viola's, Orsino's, Malvolio's).
- Its constant concern with the difference between appearance and reality invites the audience to think about how easily people can be fooled by outward appearance.

- It directs attention to the unstable nature of language, showing that the meaning of words slip and slide.
- It prompts thought about questions of gender, most obviously in Viola's disguise as Cesario.
- Illyria's fantastic happenings have moral consequences. Brother finds sister, lovers will marry, self-centredness yields to awareness of others. Illusions are the way to find truth.
- The play offers alternative illusions (of love, happiness, self-perception, etc.), but does not endorse any, and invites you to think, consider, and choose.
- The play certainly makes entertaining theatre, but its complexity and openness to interpretation makes it much more than 'simply an entertaining comedy'. Shakespeare can entertain you and make you think at the same time!

Writing about character

As the section on Critical approaches showed, much critical writing about *Twelfth Night* traditionally focused on characters, writing about them as if they were living human beings. Today it is not sufficient just to describe their personalities. When you write about characters you will also be expected to show that they are dramatic constructs, part of Shakespeare's stagecraft. They embody the wider concerns of the play, have certain dramatic functions, and are set in a social world with particular values and beliefs. They reflect and express issues of significance to Shakespeare's society – and today's.

All that may seem difficult and abstract. But don't feel overwhelmed. Everything you read in this Guide is written with those principles in mind, and can be a model for your own writing. Of course you should say what a character seems like to you, but you should also write about how Shakespeare makes them part of his overall dramatic design.

Another way of thinking about characters is to consider that in Shakespeare's time playwrights and audiences were less concerned with psychological realism than with character types and their functions. That is, they expected and recognised such stock figures of traditional drama as the melancholy Petrarchan lover (Orsino), the drunken braggart (Sir Toby), the dupe or gull (Sir Andrew), the pompous hypocrite who is exposed (Malvolio) and so on. Today, film and television have accustomed audiences to expect the inner life of characters to be revealed. Although Shakespeare's characters do reveal their inmost thoughts and feelings, especially in soliloquy, his audiences tended to regard them as characters in a developing story, to be understood by how they formed part of that story, and by how far they conformed to certain well-known types and fulfilled certain traditional roles.

It can be helpful to consider minor characters, whose roles are little more than functional. They are dramatic devices who briefly perform their part, then disappear from the play. The sea captain rescues Viola from the shipwreck, provides information about Orsino and Olivia, and promises to assist Viola's plan of disguise. The priest confirms the marriage of Olivia and Sebastian. Curio is little more than a 'feed' for Orsino (merely speaking to evoke his master's response), and Valentine reports Olivia's rejection of Orsino's wooing, and is used to convey the information that Viola has become Orsino's favourite courtier. Although actors playing these minor roles can create a vivid sense of personality, they exist only for certain particular dramatic purposes. In contrast, major characters have more extensive dramatic functions, and actors have far greater opportunities to create the stage illusion of a real person.

But there is also a danger in writing about the functions of characters or the character types they represent. To reduce a character to a mere plot device is just as inappropriate as treating them as a real person. When you write about characters in *Twelfth Night* you should try to achieve a balance between analysing their personality, identifying the dilemmas they face, showing how they change or develop in the course of the play, and placing them in their social, critical and dramatic contexts. That style of writing is found all through this Guide, and that, together with the following brief discussions, can help your own written responses to character.

Orsino can be regarded as a conventional romantic character type: the melancholy Petrarchan lover of a woman who rejects and disdains his love. Lovesick, moody and poetical, he indulges his emotions; his high-flown language and fantasies about Olivia suggest that he is more in love with the idea of love than with an actual living woman. As such, he embodies a central concern of the play: the failure to distinguish illusion from reality, and that failure to see things as they are makes him appear posturing and absurd. It is often argued that the play charts his progress to emotional maturity as, through Viola, he breaks free of illusion and finds true love with her. But an alternative interpretation is that Shakespeare continues to insist on the folly of romantic, self-deluding love by giving Orsino a final line about Viola which suggests that he merely substitutes one fantasy for another: 'Orsino's mistress, and his fancy's queen'.

Olivia can be interpreted, within the design of the play, as Orsino's counterpart. Shakespeare shows that, like Orsino, Olivia also mistakes illusion for reality. Her illusions, like his, cannot be sustained, and as they are stripped away, have comic results. The illusion that she can shut herself away from the world for seven years to mourn her brother is quickly dispelled as she enjoys Feste's joking, then is almost instantly infatuated by the disguised Viola. Misled by outward appearances, she mistakes infatuation for love, but like Orsino's love, hers too proves sentimental and self-deceiving. Shakespeare shows the follies of such love as Olivia equates love with sickness ('Even so quickly may one catch the plague?'), resorts to the subterfuge of sending her ring after Viola, and quickly marries Sebastian, unable to recognise he is not Cesario. But in his portrayal of Olivia, Shakespeare balances her self-deceptions against her evident qualities. She is a capable mistress of her household, possesses a wry humour, and towards the play's end, as she expresses concern for Malvolio's well-being ('poor gentleman'), she sees clearly that she too has been in the grip of 'A most extracting frenzy'.

Malvolio can be interpreted as Shakespeare's dramatic representation of another aspect of the folly that results from self-regarding love. Olivia's condemnation 'O you are sick of self-love, Malvolio', and Maria's declaration 'it is his grounds of faith that all that look on him love him' precisely identify the illusions that will bring about Malvolio's humiliation. His fantasies, conceit, vanity and sense of superiority bring him low as he all too easily falls for the device of the forged letter. But although Malvolio, like other characters, is a dramatic portrayal of the folly that arises from delusion, such a complex character cannot be reduced to a single functional interpretation. He has also been seen as representative of puritan killjoy disapproval of 'cakes and ale' festivity, and as a dramatic portrayal of the emerging class in Shakespeare's England that threatened aristocratic privilege and power. His final threat of revenge has sometimes been interpreted as a foreshadowing of the English Civil War 40 years later and the closure of the theatres.

Further, in spite of his disdain, arrogance, intolerance, pretensions and pomposity (and the implications of his name, Malvolio = 'ill-will'), he is an efficient and conscientious steward, and his humiliating treatment as a madman makes modern audiences increasingly uncomfortable.

Sir Toby Belch and **Sir Andrew Aguecheek** link the love plot and the comic plot. They are recognisable characters rooted in dramatic tradition and social values. Sir Toby derives from the boastful, drunken braggart. His name, Belch, suggests his earthy disposition, and his behaviour in the play makes him represent the spirit of Twelfth Night: hedonistic enjoyment, cakes and ale, revelling and rejection of constraint. Sir Andrew is the traditional gull, a rich ninny whose foolishness renders him all too available to be fleeced and cheated by Sir Toby. Like other characters, Sir Andrew is in the grip of illusion. He thinks of himself as a lover, a scholar and a skilled duellist, but each self-perception is comically exposed as a delusion. Shakespeare ensures that both characters display varied features of character that complicate audience response. Sir Toby is a bully, a cheat, a liar and a cruel practical joker. He is also, like Malvolio, a hypocrite, because for all his anti-authoritarian revelling he is acutely conscious of his own social position as a relative of the high-status Olivia. But he is also brave and witty, and his melancholy echoes Orsino's. Sir Andrew, for all his witlessness and lack of originality of thought, has one of the most endearing lines in the play which suggests he may now have become yet another of the play's melancholy lovers: 'I was adored once, too.' The final appearance of the two knights, in which Sir Toby contemptuously dismisses Andrew's offer of help, can inject a strong note of pathos.

Maria plays a key part in Malvolio's humiliation. Her language and actions show her to be witty and intelligent, but stage productions vary widely in how they present her. Occasionally she is played as a gentlewoman of quite high status, but more often her social status seems much lower. Sometimes she is presented as sincerely in love with Sir Toby, but a few productions have played her as a calculating schemer, obviously planning to improve her social position by marrying Toby.

Viola is conventionally interpreted as representing a contrast to all other characters in the play who are deceived by appearances. Unlike them, she is not in the grip of illusion, and her dramatic function is to lead Olivia and Orsino out of their illusions and help them realise what true love can really be, turning away from self-indulgent and self-deceiving love. Virtually all interpretations agree that Viola represents selfless love in the play. She is not self-seeking but self-sacrificing, and the plot device of disguise enables Shakespeare to suggest great complexity in her character. She woos another woman on behalf of the man she loves, and is willing even to die if Orsino so wishes it. She speaks simply and directly about her love in language which is not affected, but sincere. But Shakespeare complicates his presentation of her character. Like Olivia, Viola falls quickly in love, but is she also deceived by appearances? Just what does she see in the evidently self-centred, posturing Orsino, a man who does not know what true love is? And for all her clear-sightedness, in one episode Viola's response is merely a device to fulfil the demands of the comic plot: she must be fooled into thinking that Sir Andrew is a formidable duellist: 'a devil in private brawl'.

Feste links the love plot and the comic plots of the play, moving freely between Olivia's household and Orsino's palace, and accepted as a companion in Sir Toby's revels. He is an emblem of the folly that runs through the play. He is a shrewd observer, a licensed fool whose dramatic function is to comment caustically on the behaviour of his social superiors. Only Malvolio resents his foolery, and Feste takes a harsh revenge on the overbearing steward. Feste delights in wordplay. He puns, riddles, engages in repartee, invents mock-logical arguments and high-sounding but fake authorities (Quinapalus, and the old hermit of Prague), offers mock-religious advice, and seizes any opportunity to create nonsense from words. His language demonstrates how meanings shift constantly in the topsy-turvy world of Illyria. He provides an ironic description of much of the play: 'Foolery, sir, does walk about the orb like the sun; it shines everywhere.' To Elizabethans, he may have seemed unproblematic, fitting within well-known dramatic conventions of the clown (see page 66). But today he is viewed as an enigmatic figure, insecure and melancholy, a satirist and an opportunist, and directly critical of Viola: 'I do not care for you'. In many nineteenth- and early twentieth-century productions, Feste was played as little more than a merry, well-intentioned fool, but increasingly in the second half of the twentieth century and in the twenty-first, his presentation has been more troubled and morose. Directors have been concerned to emphasise how the style and content of his songs and comments help bring out the less cheering complexities of the play.

A note on examiners

Examiners do not try to trap you or trick you. They set questions and select passages for comment intended to help you write your own informed personal response to the play. They expect your answer to display a sound knowledge and understanding of the play, and to be well structured. They want you to develop an argument, using evidence from the text to support your interpretations and judgements. Examiners know there is never one 'right answer' to a question, but always opportunities to explore different approaches and interpretations. As such, they welcome answers which directly address the question set, and which demonstrate originality, insight and awareness of complexity. Above all, they reward responses which show your perception that *Twelfth Night* is a play for performance, and that you can identify how Shakespeare achieves his dramatic effects.

And what about critics? Examiners want you to show you are aware of different critical approaches to the play. But they do not expect you simply to drop critics' names into your essay, or to remember quotations from critics. Rather, they want you to show that you can interpret the play from different critical perspectives, and that you know that any critical approach provides only a partial view of *Twelfth Night*. Often, that need only be just a section of your essay. Examiners are always interested in *your* view of the play. They expect your writing to show how you have come to that view from thinking critically about the play, reading it, seeing it performed, reading about it, and perhaps from acting some of it yourself – even if that acting is in your imagination!

Resources

Books

C L Barber, *Shakespeare's Festive Comedy*, Princeton University Press, 1959
An important critical study that explores how the social form of Elizabethan holidays contributed to the dramatic form of Shakespeare's comedies. The chapter on *Twelfth Night* focuses on misrule and the folly of time-serving.

Harold Bloom, *Shakespeare: The Invention of the Human*, Fourth Estate, 1999
Although the book is censured by most modern critics, Bloom's chapter on *Twelfth Night* is a thought-provoking example of detailed character study.

M C Bradbrook, 'Robert Armin and *Twelfth Night*' in D J Palmer (ed.), *Shakespeare: Twelfth Night, A Casebook*, see below.
Argues that Shakespeare created Feste as a wise fool because a new actor, Robert Armin, joined his acting company to play clown roles.

A C Bradley, 'Feste the Jester' in D J Palmer (ed.), *Shakespeare: Twelfth Night, A Casebook*, see below.
An essay in character criticism which, reacting to Victorian critical and performance emphasis on Malvolio and Viola, argues for the centrality of Feste in the play.

Michael D Bristol, 'The Festive Agon: The Politics of Carnival' in R S White (ed.), *New Casebooks: Twelfth Night, Contemporary Critical Essays*, see below.
Argues that *Twelfth Night* represents the political struggle between traditional power structures and the misrule that is Carnival.

John Russell Brown, *Shakespeare's Plays in Performance*, Edward Arnold, 1966
Fully alert to the rich variety of staging potentialities of the plays. The chapter on *Twelfth Night* (also in D J Palmer, below) perceptively explores solutions to the visual opportunities within the text.

Dympna Callaghan, 'And All is Semblative a Woman's Part': Body Politics and *Twelfth Night*' in R S White (ed.), *New Casebooks: Twelfth Night, Contemporary Critical Essays*, see below.
A feminist essay which argues that women are the casualties of the play, oppressed and marginalised.

H B Charlton, *Shakespearean Comedy*, Methuen, 1938
An influential book which traces in the comedies the growth of Shakespeare's 'comic idea'. The chapter arguing for the artistic unity of *Twelfth Night* is in D J Palmer (ed.), *Shakespeare: Twelfth Night, A Casebook*, see below.

Terry Eagleton, *William Shakespeare*, Basil Blackwell, 1986
Although Eagleton includes only a few pages on *Twelfth Night*, his book exemplifies postmodern (or deconstructive) approaches to Shakespeare's plays.

Harley Granville Barker, *Prefaces to Shakespeare: Love's Labour's Lost, Twelfth Night, The Merchant of Venice*, Batsford, 1982
A highly influential reading by a theatre practitioner. Essential for students of stagecraft. Granville Barker, himself a playwright and director, gives prescriptive advice on staging and characterisation.

Geoffrey H Hartman, 'Shakespeare's Poetical Character in *Twelfth Night*' in R S White (ed.), *New Casebooks: Twelfth Night, Contemporary Critical Essays*, see below.
An example of a deconstructive approach which argues against attempts to find unity in Shakespeare's plays, and uses examples from *Twelfth Night* to argue for the arbitrariness of its language.

Leslie Hotson, *The First Night of Twelfth Night*, Rupert Hart-Davis, 1954
Hotson's much-disputed argument is that Shakespeare wrote the play for a performance on Twelfth Night 1601 at Whitehall palace before Queen Elizabeth and her guest the Duke of Bracciano, Don Virginio Orsino.

Harold Jenkins, 'Shakespeare's *Twelfth Night*' in Kenneth Muir (ed.), *Shakespeare: The Comedies*, Prentice Hall, 1965
Rejects the notion that Malvolio is the centre of the play. Argues that Malvolio's folly and self-deception reflect that of Olivia and Orsino.

Frank Kermode, *Shakespeare's Language*, Allen Lane, Penguin, 2000
A detailed examination of how Shakespeare's language changed over the course of his playwriting career. Contains only a brief section on *Twelfth Night*, but the discussion of other plays can also illuminate understanding of Shakespeare's use of language in *Twelfth Night*.

Elliot Krieger, *A Marxist Study of Shakespeare's Comedies*, Macmillan, 1979
An approach to the comedies through social class and ideology. The chapter on *Twelfth Night*, 'The Morality of Indulgence', is reprinted in R S White (ed.), *New Casebooks: Twelfth Night, Contemporary Critical Essays*, see below.

Russ McDonald, *Shakespeare and the Arts of Language*, Oxford University Press, 2001
This valuable guide to Shakespeare's language includes discussion of a number of passages from *Twelfth Night*.

D J Palmer (ed.), *Shakespeare: Twelfth Night, A Casebook*, Macmillan, 1972
Contains a valuable collection of critical writing on the play from 1602–1969, including the essays by Bradley and Bradbrook, and a selection from Charlton, noted in this booklist.

Michael Pennington, *Twelfth Night: A User's Guide*, Nick Hern Books, 2000
A detailed, practical introduction by an actor who has directed three productions of the play. Very readable, with many theatrical insights.

Bruce R Smith (ed.), *Twelfth Night: Texts and Contexts*, Palgrave, 2001
Contains a selection of documents and illustrations from early modern England. Topics represented include: romance, music, sexuality, clothing and disguise, household economies, Puritan probity, clowning and laughter.

Caroline Spurgeon, *Shakespeare's Imagery and What it Tells Us*, Cambridge University Press, 1935
The first major study of imagery in the plays. Although much criticised today, Spurgeon's identification of image-clusters as a dominant feature of the plays has influenced later studies.

Leonard Tennenhouse, 'Power on Display: The Politics of Shakespeare's Genres', in R S White (ed.), *New Casebooks: Twelfth Night, Contemporary Critical Essays*, see below.
A feminist approach which argues that female desire is the driving force of *Twelfth Night*, even though, through marriage, power returns to men at the end.

R S White (ed.), *New Casebooks: Twelfth Night, Contemporary Critical Essays*, Macmillan, 1996
A collection of essays representative of recent critical approaches to the play (political, feminist, deconstructive). Contains the essays by Bristol, Callaghan, Hartman, Krieger and Tennenhouse noted in this booklist.

Films

A film of *Twelfth Night*, directed by Yakov Fried, was made in the USSR in 1955, but is no longer available. A half-hour animated version, adapted by Leon Garfield, is available in the Animated Tales series. The two versions that can usually be obtained on video are:

Twelfth Night (UK, 1979) Director: John Gorrie. Felicity Kendall (Viola/Cesario); Alec McCowen (Malvolio).
Made for the BBC/Time-Life series, this television version uses Elizabethan-Jacobean costumes and settings.

Twelfth Night (UK, 1996) Director: Trevor Nunn. Imogen Stubbs (Viola/Cesario); Nigel Hawthorne (Malvolio).
Set in the 1890s, Nunn's film opens with the shipwreck of a cruise liner on which Viola and Sebastian are cross-dressing entertainers. Filmed in Cornwall with St Michael's Mount as Orsino's castle.

Audio books

Four major versions are easily available, in the series by Naxos, Arkangel, Harper-Collins and BBC Radio Collection.

Twelfth Night on the Web

If you type 'Twelfth Night Shakespeare' into your search engine, it will find around 60,000 items. Because websites are of wildly varying quality, and rapidly disappear or are created, no recommendation can safely be made here. But if you have time to browse, you may find much of interest.